Open Cour Reading

D0597765

Reading and Writing Workbook

Program Authors

Carl Bereiter
Marilyn Jager Adams
Michael Pressley
Marsha Roit
Robbie Case
Anne McKeough
Jan Hirshberg
Marlene Scardamalia
Ann Brown
Joe Campione
Iva Carruthers
Gerald H. Treadway, Jr.

A Division of The McGraw·Hill Companies

Columbus, Ohio

SRA/McGraw-Hill

A Division of The McGraw·Hill Companies

Copyright © 2000 by SRA/McGraw-Hill.

All rights reserved. Except as permitted under the United States
Copyright Act, no part of this publication may be reproduced or
distributed in any form or by any means, or stored in a database
or retrieval system, without the prior written permission of the
publisher, unless otherwise indicated.

Send all inquiries to:
SRA/McGraw-Hill
8787 Orion Place
Columbus, Ohio 43240

Printed in the United States of America.

ISBN 0-02-831065-9

19 20 21 22 23 DBH 09 08 07 06 05

Table *of* Contents

Unit 5

Unit 6

Compare and Contrast

Come Back, Jack!

Focus Writers sometimes use comparison in a story to make an idea clearer and to make the story more interesting for the reader.

- To **compare** means to tell how things, events, or characters are **alike** in some way.

- To **contrast** means to tell how things, events, or characters are **different**.

- To help show how things are alike and different, use clue words like the following:

Clue Words

Alike		**Different**
both	as	different
same	too	but
like		

Practice Decide if the following sentences are comparing or contrasting. Circle the correct answer. Then on the line write the clue word.

1. Jack loved books, but his sister did not.

Compare (Contrast) __but_____

2. Jack and his sister both liked games.

(Compare) Contrast __both_____

3. Jack went into the castle. Jill went in the castle too.

   Compare   Contrast   _____

4. The little girl laughed, just like Jack.

   Compare   Contrast   _____

Apply Think about "Come Back, Jack!" List two ways that Jack and his sister are alike.

1. _____

   _____

2. _____

   _____

List two ways that Jack and his sister are different.

3. _____

   _____

4. _____

   _____

Figurative Language

Focus Writers use words to help readers think about something common in a new way. They often use figurative language to do this.

- Writers can compare one thing to another using the word *like*.

    Jack wriggled <u>like</u> a worm.

    His sister ran <u>like</u> the wind.

- Writers can also compare things by using the word *as*.

    The giant was <u>as</u> big <u>as</u> a tree.

    The children were <u>as</u> quiet <u>as</u> mice.

Practice Read each sentence. Circle the words that tell you that two things are being compared.

1. Jack fell like a rock.

2. Jill's eyes were as big as saucers.

3. The giant's voice sounded like thunder.

4. He felt as hungry as a horse.

5. The children ran like the wind.

6. They were as playful as puppies.

7. The book was as heavy as a brick.

8. Jack jumped like a kangaroo.

9. The plum was as big as a baseball.

10. The kite flew like a bird.

Apply Compare some things yourself! Write a word to finish each sentence.

1. The cereal tasted like _____.

2. My friend is as funny as _____.

3. I ran as fast as _____.

4. The banana felt like _____.

5. The kitten felt as soft as _____.

6. These shoes are as big as _____.

7. The kitchen smells like _____.

8. This new flavor tastes like _____.

9. The moon was as bright as _____.

10. The snow was as deep as _____.

Position Words

Focus Writers use position words to help the reader get a better idea of where things are.

- Position words are also called words of place and location.

- Position words often answer questions that start with *where*.

- Some position words you may see are:

above	over	in front of	next to
on top of	below	beneath	under
near	inside	outside	beside

Practice Look through "Come Back, Jack!" for sentences that contain position, or place and location words. Write one example on the lines below. Circle the words that show position.

_____

_____

_____

_____

Look at each picture and read the question.
Write a sentence that answers the question.

1. Where are the shoes?

_____

2. Where is the puppy sleeping?

_____

3. Where is the flag?

_____

Apply Write a sentence that tells where
something (a wastebasket, a pencil sharpener, a
map, a bulletin board) is in the classroom. Use
position words to make your description clear.

_____

_____

_____

Name _____ Date _____

Nouns

Focus Language is made up of different kinds of words called **parts of speech**. Nouns are one part of speech.

- A noun can name a **person.**
  The <u>man</u> wore a hat.

- A noun can name a **place.**
  Do you have your own <u>bedroom</u>?

- A noun can name a **thing.**
  I rode on the <u>bus</u>.

Practice Underline the word in each sentence that is the kind of noun listed on the left.

1. person The boy went to a party.

2. place   I saw a cow in the barn.

3. thing   Where is my book?

4. thing   He saw a pond.

5. place   The girl walked in the park.

6. person Rain fell on the boy.

7. place   The elephant danced at the circus.

8. thing   The window is stuck.

9. place   We went to the zoo.

10. person   The girl played a game.

Apply Complete each sentence. Write a word
that is the kind of noun listed to the left.

1. (person)   _____ likes to read funny stories.

2. (place)   Yesterday we went to the _____.

3. (thing)   Where is my _____?

4. (person)   Do you know _____?

5. (person)   _____ wore a coat to school.

6. (thing)   He liked the red _____.

7. (place)   We walked to the _____.

8. (thing)   I gave a _____ to Aunt Betty.

9. (person)   _____ hit a baseball.

10. (place)   I had fun at the _____.

Following Clues
(Making Inferences)

Focus Sometimes a writer does not tell the reader everything. Sometimes a writer leaves clues for the reader to follow.

- Information in a story gives the reader a clue.

- Clues can help you learn more about a story's characters. For example, *Gwen put on her golden crown.* You can figure out from this sentence that Gwen is probably a queen or princess.

Identify Read each sentence below. Then look in "Story Hour—Starring Megan!" for clues that help you know the characters better.

1. Megan really wants to learn to read. What clue tells you?

   _____

2. Megan knew Andrew was there before she saw him. What clue tells you?

   _____

Practice and Apply Read the paragraphs
below. Then answer the questions.

Megan takes Alfred for a walk every day.
When they get home, Megan feeds and waters
Alfred. Then she brushes his shiny fur. Alfred
barks his thanks.

What is Alfred? _____

What clues tell you that? _____

_____

_____

Yesterday, Bert had trouble getting to
school on time. First, he could not find his
boots. Then, he could not find his mittens.
When he finally got his coat, hat, and scarf
on, the bus was waiting for him.

What is the weather like? _____

What clues tell you that? _____

_____

_____

Characters Think and Feel
(Characterization)

Focus In stories, the author tells us what characters think and feel in order to make the characters more interesting.

- Writers often tell us what a character is thinking or feeling.

- This helps us better understand that character and the story.
  Megan would sigh, "Oh, reading is so hard!"

Identify Look in "Story Hour—Starring Megan!" for an example of how Megan feels about Andrew. Discuss the examples with your classmates.

Sentence that tells how Megan feels about Andrew:

_____

_____

_____

Practice and Apply Read the story, then write your answers to each question.

> Tony had to give a report at school.
>
> "I don't like speaking in front of the whole class," Tony said to his mother.
>
> Later, Mrs. O'Brien announced, "The next report is by Tony Perez."
>
> Tony walked to the front of the class. He began his report. He thought his voice was too loud. He thought his knees were shaking. But he remembered his whole report!
>
> "Very good job, Tony," Mrs. O'Brien said.
>
> "I'm so proud of you!" said his mother.
>
> "Giving reports is fun!" said Tony.

1. What did Mrs. O'Brien think of Tony's report?

_____

2. How did Tony's mother feel about him?

_____

3. How did Tony feel about speaking in front of the class before he made his report?

_____

4. How did Tony feel about speaking in front of the class after he made his report?

_____

Regular Plurals

Focus Plural nouns name more than one person, place, or thing.

> - Most nouns can be made plural by adding -s or -es. *Day* means one day. *Days* means more than one day.
> - Words that end in *s, ss, x, ch,* and *sh* are made plural by adding -es. More than one dish would be *dishes.*

Practice Make each word below plural.

1. book _____

2. pass _____

3. bench _____

4. dinosaur _____

5. letter _____

Use the words above in the sentences that follow. Sometimes you will use the plural noun. Sometimes you will not.

6. Andrew had many toy _____.

7. Megan wanted to read all of the _____ in the library.

8. The children sat on a _____.

9. Words are made up of _____.

10. Do you have any movie _____?

Apply Write two sentences using each of these nouns. In the first sentence, do not make the noun plural. In the second sentence, make it plural.

pencil	picture	glass

1. _____

_____

2. _____

_____

3. _____

_____

4. _____

_____

5. _____

_____

6. _____

_____

Multisyllabic words

Focus Many words are made up of more than one syllable.

Here are some guidelines to help figure out long words.

- Put a dot under each vowel or vowel cluster (two or more vowels together), except for words with the silent *e*. This will tell you how many syllables are in the word. Then using letter sounds, sound out each syllable.

  almost   decode   hungry

- Look in a dictionary or glossary.

Practice Place a dot under each vowel or cluster in the words below. On the line, write how many syllables the word has.

1. angry   _____ syllables

2. recall   _____ syllables

3. almost   _____ syllables

4. before   _____ syllables

5. tomorrow   _____ syllables

6. October   _____ syllables

7. summer _____ syllables

8. doctor _____ syllables

9. later _____ syllables

10. library _____ syllables

11. dinosaur _____ syllables

12. purple _____ syllables

13. September _____ syllables

14. Saturday _____ syllables

15. education _____ syllables

Apply Write three sentences below. Use at least one multisyllabic word in each sentence.

1. _____

_____

2. _____

_____

3. _____

_____

Verbs

Focus A verb is a part of speech. Every sentence has a verb.

> Some verbs are action verbs. They tell what is, was, or will be happening.
>> Megan <u>waters</u> the plants in the library.
>> I <u>threw</u> the ball to Jamal.

Practice Read each sentence. Circle the verbs.

1. I read a book at bedtime.

2. He saw a brown bear.

3. The dog barked at night.

4. She ate seven lollipops.

5. Kevin rides a bike.

6. Red cars race around the track.

7. The kittens run across the room.

8. Grace fills a bucket with water.

Apply Find a verb in the box to complete the sentence. Then write the verb on the line.

baked	watched
ate	saved
wrote	turned
write	grew
learned	played
read	climbs

1. Yesterday I _____ a cake.

2. Megan _____ her baby brother.

3. The bananas _____ yellow.

4. I _____ with a pencil.

5. We _____ about verbs.

6. Nathan _____ with his friends.

Author's Purpose

Focus Writers have a purpose or reason for writing. They decide what they want their writing to do for the reader.

- One purpose authors have for writing is to teach something or give information. *An ant is an insect* gives information.

- Another purpose authors have for writing is to entertain. *Alfred the ant could not carry the heavy crumb* is written for your enjoyment.

Identify Think about the story "Ant and the Three Little Figs" as you answer these questions.

1. What was the author's purpose for writing the story?

_____

2. How do you know?

_____

_____

_____

Practice Read each sentence. Write I if it gives information or teaches you something. Write E if it entertains or makes you laugh.

1. ___ Pigs are farm animals.

2. ___ Figs are fruits.

3. ___ The three little figs met a big bad lemon.

4. ___ The big bad watermelon asked the three little bananas for a cup of sugar.

5. ___ Figs grow in California.

Apply Write a paragraph about any animal. Decide if you want the story to give information or entertain.

_____

_____

_____

_____

_____

_____

_____

_____

Mood and Tone

Focus Good writers often create a mood, or feeling, for a story in order to keep the readers interested. A story's mood can be cheerful, sad, funny, or scary. Tone reflects the attitude of the characters and how they act with each other. The tone can be friendly, angry, curious, or understanding.

Writers create **mood** through
- descriptive words
- setting
- what characters do
- what characters say
- illustrations

Practice Think about the story "Ant and the Three Little Figs." Look at the sentence or phrase below. Explain how each helps to set the mood.

Sentence or phrase	How it helps create mood
I like to read. I said "Okay."	_____ _____
The Ant waited, too.	_____ _____

Look at the phrases below. Tell what kind of
tone each creates.

Phrase   **What kind of tone it creates**

*"No! Don't
do that!..."*   _____

                            _____

"Where are you   _____
going, Ant?..."
                            _____

He said, "But   _____
thank you for
reading to me."   _____

Apply Write a paragraph about two people.
Use descriptive phrases to set the mood. Use
dialogue to show the tone.

_____

_____

_____

_____

_____

_____

Letter Patterns

Focus Knowing common letter patterns, or phonograms, and their pronunciation can help you read and spell many unfamiliar words.

- A phonogram is a letter pattern that has a vowel sound plus a consonant. A phonogram needs a beginning consonant to make it a word.

- Some common phonograms are

-at	-ead	-ide	-og	-uff
-ack	-ell	-ig	-ot	-ug
-ad	-ed	-ime	-ock	-um
-amp	-end	-ight	-od	-ut
-and	-ent	-ink	-op	-ub

Practice Look through selections you have read to find one word for each of the following phonograms.

-ack	-at	-ig	-ide	-ad
_____	_____	_____	_____	_____

-ent	-ight	-ime	-ut	-ot
_____	_____	_____	_____	_____

Write four words for each of the following
phonograms.

1. -and   _____   _____   _____   _____

2. -ent   _____   _____   _____   _____

3. -ink   _____   _____   _____   _____

4. -op   _____   _____   _____   _____

5. -ub   _____   _____   _____   _____

Apply Choose some of the words you have
written to write a silly poem on the lines below.

_____

_____

_____

_____

_____

_____

_____

Compound Words

Focus Sometimes two words are put together to make new words that have different meanings. These new words are called compound words.

Here are examples of compound words:
star + fish	becomes	starfish
house + work	becomes	housework
grand + mother	becomes	grandmother
class + room	becomes	classroom

Practice Draw a line from one word in the first column to one word in the second column to make a compound word. Use each word only once.

1. sail   plane

2. rain   cake

3. air   book

4. paint   boat

5. cup   bow

6. news   brush

7. note   paper

Apply Make compound words out of the two
words on each of the following lines. Then write
a sentence for each compound word.

1. dog house _____

_____

_____

2. cow boy _____

_____

_____

3. bed room _____

_____

_____

4. sand box _____

_____

_____

Name _____ Date _____

Pronouns

*Ant and the Three
Little Figs*

Focus Pronouns are words that take the place of nouns. Using the right pronoun makes your meaning clear. The nouns that the pronouns take the place of are called *antecedents*.

- A **singular** (one) **pronoun** takes the place of a singular noun.
  Joey played ball. He had a good time.

- **Plural** (more than one) **pronouns** take the place of plural nouns.
  Joey and Celia played ball. They had fun.

Practice Underline the pronouns in the following sentences. Circle the noun or nouns that each pronoun replaces.

1. Betsy lost her kitten.

2. Mark placed his book on the table.

3. This window is stuck. Please close it.

4. Kyle is ready. When will Uncle Bill meet him?

5. Did Max bake the cake? It is good.

6. The books are about animals. They have lots of pictures.

7. Will Mike and Liz drive when they take a trip?

Reading and Writing Workbook • *Pronouns and Antecedents*   **35**

Read each numbered sentence. Place an X next to the sentence below it that uses the correct pronoun to replace the underlined word.

8. The <u>squirrels</u> watched the dog.

_____ They watched the dog.

_____ It watched the dog.

9. The <u>sunset</u> was beautiful.

_____ It was beautiful.

_____ She was beautiful.

Apply In the sentences below, the pronouns do not match their antecedents. The antecedents are underlined. Draw a line through each incorrect pronoun. Write the correct pronoun above it.

1. <u>Mrs. Rabbit</u> gathered carrots. He fed the carrots to the bunnies.

2. <u>Ralph and Tim</u> have a pet mouse. He took the mouse to school.

3. <u>Mr. Angelo</u> wants to go to the party. It has a present for Beth.

4. <u>Scott and I</u> went hiking. She spent the day on a trail.

Viewpoint of a Story

Focus A viewpoint is the way the events of a story are described. Stories are told from a character's viewpoint or from the author's viewpoint.

- When a story is written from a character's viewpoint, readers see the story through the eyes of that character. The sentence *I went to the library* is written from Tomás's viewpoint.

- An author's viewpoint gives information about the story through the eyes of someone who is not part of the story. The sentence *Tomás went to the library* is written from the author's viewpoint.

Practice Find your favorite book. Fill in the spaces below.

Title: _____

Story's viewpoint: _____

How do you know who is telling this story?

_____

_____

Apply Write a short paragraph about something that happened in school from a writer's viewpoint. Then rewrite the paragraph from the viewpoint of one of the characters. Perhaps you could use your teacher's viewpoint.

_____

_____

_____

_____

_____

_____

_____

_____

_____

_____

Name _____ Date _____

Setting

Focus Writers describe the setting of a story to give readers a better picture of when and where the story takes place.

> The **setting** of a story is the time and place in which the story happens.

Identify Look in "Tomás and the Library Lady" for examples of when and where things take place. Write them below.

Page: _____

Sentences that tell **when** something happens:

_____

_____

_____

Page: _____

Sentences that tell **where** something happens:

_____

_____

_____

Practice and Apply Read the story and answer the questions. Then describe the setting in your own words.

Our scout troop went for a hike in a forest last summer. The trees were so thick that it was dark, even in the morning! Not one ray of sunlight could get through those trees. Sometimes we couldn't even see the trail, so we carefully followed the forest ranger who acted as our guide. The ranger told us lots of interesting things about the forest and the animals living there. I think that I may become a forest ranger when I grow up!

1. When did this story take place?

_____

2. Where did this story take place?

_____

3. Describe the setting in your own words.

_____

_____

Adding *-ed*, *-ing* Endings

Focus Adding *-ed* and *-ing* to verbs makes new words.

> • For most one-syllable words with a short vowel and one final consonant, double the final consonant and add *-ed* or *-ing*.
>
> • For verbs ending in a consonant followed by *y*, change *y* to *i* to add *-ed*. No change is needed to add *-ing*.
>
> • For verbs ending in a consonant followed by *e*, drop the *e* to add *-ed* or *-ing*.

Practice Add *-ed* and *-ing* to each of the words listed below.

Verb	Add *-ed*	Add *-ing*
carry	_____	_____
stop	_____	_____
watch	_____	_____
climb	_____	_____
laugh	_____	_____

Use the new verbs to complete these sentences.

1. The car _____ when Tomás and his family reached Iowa.

2. Children came out of the library _____
books.

3. Tomás started _____ the
stairs to the library.

4. Tomás _____ the library
lady take some books from the shelves.

5. The library lady _____ as
Tomás flapped his arms.

Apply Write your own sentences using the
other words from the **Practice** activity.

1. _____

_____

2. _____

_____

3. _____

_____

4. _____

_____

5. _____

_____

Antonyms

Focus Antonyms are words that mean the
opposite or nearly the opposite of each other.

Here are a few antonyms:

big	little
loud	soft
here	there
go	come

Practice Match each word on the left with its
antonym on the right.

_____ **1.** hot   **a.** dark

_____ **2.** short   **b.** empty

_____ **3.** in   **c.** cold

_____ **4.** full   **d.** bad

_____ **5.** up   **e.** pretty

_____ **6.** light   **f.** tall

_____ **7.** happy   **g.** sad

_____ **8.** good   **h.** down

_____ **9.** ugly   **i.** thin

_____ **10.** fat   **j.** out

Apply Pick some words from stories you
wrote. Write them under **Word.** Under
Antonym, write an antonym for each word. **Answers will vary.**

Word	Antonym
_____	_____
_____	_____
_____	_____
_____	_____
_____	_____
_____	_____

How would the meaning of your stories change
if you used the antonyms?

_____

_____

_____

_____

_____

_____

Adjectives

Focus An adjective describes or tells more
about a noun or pronoun.

> Writers use adjectives to help paint a picture
> in the reader's mind.
>
> > I bought a **red** coat.

Practice Circle the adjective and underline
the noun it describes.

1. The car is old.

2. The hot sun melted the ice.

3. We drove by a tall mountain.

4. They will pick the ripe corn.

5. The cool water tastes good.

Write a sentence for each adjective. Underline
the noun it describes.

6. round _____

   _____

7. tired _____

   _____

Apply Write an adjective on the line in each sentence.

1. He has _____ sisters.

2. The _____ building is next to the school.

3. The _____ bike is hers.

4. Put the _____ flowers in the vase.

5. The _____ fish swam away.

Write an adjective for each noun and use the words in a sentence.

6. _____ clown

_____

_____

7. _____ horse

_____

_____

8. _____ sky

_____

_____

Main Idea and Details

Focus Each paragraph in a story has a main idea. The detail sentences in the paragraph tell more about the main idea.

> - A **main idea** is what a paragraph is about. It is the big idea in a paragraph.
>
> - Writers use **detail sentences** to give information about the main idea.

Practice Read each main idea below. Then cross out the one sentence that does not give information about the main idea.

Main idea: Sequoyah was good at many things.

Sequoyah was a warrior, hunter, trader, and silversmith.
Sequoyah was raised Cherokee.
Sequoyah knew several languages, so he was also an interpreter.

Main idea: The Cherokee alphabet

Sequoyah was born around 1770.
At first, Sequoyah tried using pictures for each word or idea.
Sequoyah began work on a Cherokee alphabet in 1809.

Apply Write a paragraph about Sequoyah from what you learned in this story. Make sure you have a main idea. Make sure your detail sentences tell more about the main idea.

_____

_____

_____

_____

_____

_____

_____

Short Vowels *a, e*

Focus Vowels are special letters because
they each have a long sound and a short sound.

- Short *a* has the sound heard in the following
  words: act   lamb   cat   map   glad
- Short *e* has the sound heard in the following
  words: end   hen   tell   next   pet

Practice Circle the two words in each line that
have the same short *a* or short *e* sound.

1.	cup	map	moon	cap
2.	bed	ball	baby	red
3.	they	ten	men	girl
4.	cat	mop	sat	cut
5.	fun	land	hen	hand
6.	nest	fast	sun	test
7.	top	hen	den	ham
8.	ran	big	bug	pan
9.	ant	wet	let	got
10.	sit	bad	rug	mad

Apply Follow the clues to guess each word.
Write the word on the line.

1. This word has a short *e* sound.
It rhymes with *den.*
You can write with it. _____

2. This word has a short *a* sound.
It rhymes with *hat.*
It is the name of an animal. _____

3. This word has a short *a* sound.
It rhymes with *ran.*
People cook in it. _____

4. This word has a short *e* sound.
It rhymes with *let.*
Something used to catch fish. _____

5. This word has a short *a* sound.
It rhymes with *cat.*
You put it on your head. _____

6. This word has a short *e* sound.
It rhymes with *hen.*
It is a number. _____

7. This word has a short *e* sound.
It rhymes with *best.*
A bird lives in it. _____

8. This word has a short *a* sound.
It rhymes with *land.*
It is a part of the body. _____

Headings and Captions

Focus Writers use headings and captions to organize nonfiction selections.

- **Headings** are short titles for sections in nonfiction writing. The heading tells what the section is about.

- **Captions** are short descriptions that appear with and explain pictures.

Practice Look through "Sequoyah: Inventor of the Cherokee Written Language" for one example of a heading. Write the heading and then write what the section is about. Then find one example of a caption. Write the caption and then tell what the caption tells about the picture.

1. Heading: _____

2. What is the section about? _____

_____

3. Caption: _____

4. What the caption tells about the picture: _____

_____

Apply Write a heading for each passage.

People are interested in weather. Every day they listen to the radio, watch television, and read newspapers to find out what kind of weather they can expect.

1. Heading: _____

Many famous writers have used "pen names." Pen names are names the writers use that are not their real names. Some writers who used pen names are Mark Twain, whose real name is Samuel Clemens, and Dr. Seuss, whose real name is Theodor Seuss Geisel.

2. Heading: _____

Write a caption for the picture.

3. Caption: _____

_____

Name _____   Date _____

Vowel + *r* Spellings

Focus Learning the different spellings of the vowel plus *r* sound will make your writing clearer and easier to read.

- The vowel plus *r* sound can be spelled different ways. Some spellings are:

ar	er	ear	ir	or	ur

- The spellings can have different sounds. Some sounds for each spelling are:

ar	er	ear	ir	or	ur
sh**ar**e	h**er**e	h**ear**	g**ir**l	f**or**	h**ur**ry
p**ar**k	h**er**	h**ear**d	th**ir**	w**or**k	po**ur**
	wh**er**e	b**ear**	we**ir**d		

Practice Look through "Sequoyah: Inventor of the Cherokee Written Language." Find and write words that have one of the vowel plus *r* spellings.

_____   _____   _____   _____

_____   _____   _____   _____

_____   _____   _____   _____

_____   _____   _____   _____

Look at the following list of words. Group them according to the sound made by the vowel plus *r* spelling in the word at the top of each column.

dart	more	parent	yard	fern
large	near	here	spear	nurse
share	worn	sharp	morning	hear
their	spur	pour	pear	heard

lark	**care**	**or**	**cheer**	**turn**
_____	_____	_____	_____	_____
_____	_____	_____	_____	_____
_____	_____	_____	_____	_____
_____	_____	_____	_____	_____

Apply Write riddles using words from the list above. For example: I help people when they are sick. Who am I? (*nurse*)

1. _____

_____

2. _____

_____

Homographs and Homophones

Focus A homograph is a word that has the same spelling as another word but has a different meaning.

Sequoyah: Inventor of the Cherokee Written Language

- Homographs can have the same pronunciation.

   We went to the **park.**
   You can **park** the car over here.

- Homographs can also have different pronunciations.

   I will **read** the book. I **read** it last night.

Practice and Apply Complete the sentences using **hand** or **bow**. Then write the meaning.

1. I want to hold your _____.

   _____ means _____.

2. When John fell, I gave him a _____.

   _____ means _____.

3. The gift was tied with a _____

   _____ means _____.

4. The captain stood on the ship's _____.

   _____ means _____.

Focus Homophones are words that sound the same, but have different spellings and meanings.

A homophone is a word that has the same sound as another word but has a different spelling and meaning.

We **ate** lunch.   **Eight** of us played ball.

Practice and Apply Use these homophones to complete the sentences.

hare   hair   knows   nose   so   sew   pail   pale

1. She combed her long _____.

2. The _____ hopped away.

3. He _____ what he wants to eat.

4. His _____ tells him that dinner is ready.

5. I feel _____ happy.

6. I can _____ buttons on the shirt.

7. I put sand in the _____.

8. The sick child looked _____.

Proper Nouns

Focus A proper noun is a special type of noun. Proper nouns begin with a capital letter.

> Some types of **proper nouns** are:
> - names of people, such as *Alan* and *Ellen*
> - names of places, such as *Washington* and *Australia*
> - names of things, such as book titles like *Curious George*

Practice Underline the proper noun in each sentence.

1. Pam went to the mall with her sister.

2. My family went on a trip to Hawaii.

3. The name of her favorite book is *Alice in Wonderland.*

4. Have you ever been to Canada?

5. That sweater belongs to William.

Read the sentences. Replace each pronoun with
a proper noun.

1. He went to the zoo with Steven and Anna.

_____ went to the zoo

with Steven and Anna.

2. Please give some ice cream to her.

Please give some ice cream to _____.

3. They are playing baseball.

_____ are playing baseball.

Apply Write three sentences with proper nouns in them.

1. Sentence with the name of a person

_____

_____

2. Sentence with the name of a place

_____

_____

3. Sentence with the title of a book

_____

_____

Dialogue

Focus In stories, the dialogue tells the reader exactly what the characters say.

- The quotation marks go at the beginning and end of the character's exact words.
- The speaker tag tells who said the dialogue.

"You did it!" hooted Anna.

quotation marks   speaker tag

Identify Look in "Amber on the Mountain" for examples of dialogue. Write something that Amber said, then write something that Anna said. Discuss the examples with your classmates.

Page: _____ Something that Amber said:

_____

_____

_____

Page: _____ Something that Anna said:

_____

_____

_____

Practice Read each sentence and underline the speaker tag that tells who's talking. Then put quotation marks at the beginning and end of the character's words.

1. I like the story about Amber, said Chris.

2. Aren't you glad we know how to read and write? asked Pat.

3. I think Anna was a really good teacher, Lin declared.

4. Yes! Without her, Amber still wouldn't know how to read, said Chris.

5. I don't know, said Pat. Amber did teach herself to write!

Apply Write two sentences with dialogue and quotation marks. Be sure to use a speaker tag to tell who's talking.

1. _____

_____

2. _____

_____

Name _____ Date _____

Contractions

Focus Knowing how to make and use contractions can help you to be a better writer.

- A **contraction** is one word made of two words put together. One or more letters are left out.

- An apostrophe (') takes the place of the missing letter or letters.
  I am happy to see you.
  I'm happy to see you.
  I + am = I'm

Practice Draw a line to match each pair of words with the correct contraction.

1. we are		it's
2. you are		I've
3. I have		she's
4. he is		you're
5. she will		he's
6. it is		I'll
7. I will		she'll
8. she is		we're

Apply Rewrite each sentence. Use a contraction in place of the underlined words.

1. <u>I have</u> read this book three times.

_____

_____

2. <u>You are</u> a good friend.

_____

_____

3. Our teacher said <u>we are</u> going to the museum.

_____

_____

4. The doctor said <u>I will</u> feel better tomorrow.

_____

_____

Now write a sentence of your own, using a contraction.

5. _____

_____

Words That We Use Often

Focus Many of the words that we use often do not follow the rules. They cannot be sounded out and spelled using the sounds and spellings that we learn. These words have to be learned by sight.

Some common words that do not follow the rules are:

again	only	said	do	does
other	come	enough	from	have
you	are	some	the	to
want	of	very	what	where

Practice Choose a word from the box to complete each of the following sentences.

1. He _____, "Let's play baseball!"

2. I _____ another cookie.

3. Will _____ visit us _____ soon?

4. Jill is late _____ .

5. Kit flew _____ California _____ New York last week.

6. Can Doug _____ too?

7. What _____ Sasha plan to
wear to the party?

8. Mr. Rollins told us _____ we had to

_____ for math.

Apply Circle the sight words in the word
search. Look across, down, and up for the
words. What sight words did you find?

S	B	A	G	A	I	N	X	M
O	C	R	K	L	I	S	W	D
M	O	H	U	T	T	A	A	Y
E	M	J	O	H	P	I	N	K
V	E	R	Y	E	R	D	T	L
H	Y	L	O	V	L	O	A	K
U	N	N	J	U	H	T	E	B
T	L	X	O	W	H	E	R	E
Y	I	W	D	A	D	O	E	S

Punctuating Dialogue

Focus Dialogue is what the characters say.

- Quotation marks begin and end a character's exact words.

- The speaker tag tells who is speaking.

- The first word in a quotation begins with a capital letter.

- Periods, question marks, and exclamation points go inside the quotation marks.

- A comma separates the quotation from the speaker tag and the rest of the sentence.

Practice Rewrite these sentences using quotation marks, punctuation, and capital letters.

1. I'm Amber the girl said who are you

_____

_____

2. My name is Anna the new girl answered

_____

_____

3. I will teach you to read Anna declared

_____

_____

4. The mountain girl exclaimed and I will teach
you to milk a goat

_____

_____

Apply Draw two people talking. On the lines
write the dialogue that goes with your picture.
Remember to use quotation marks, punctuation,
and capital letters.

_____

_____

_____

Drawing Conclusions

Focus Readers get ideas, or draw conclusions, about what is happening in a story by using information the writer gives them and by thinking about what they already know.

To **draw a conclusion** readers should

- look for what a writer tells about a thing, a character, or an event.

- say or write what they have learned about a thing, character, or event.

- think about what they already know.

Practice Look through "Mushroom in the Rain" to find information the writer gives about the mushroom. On the following lines write what the information tells you about mushrooms. If you already know something about mushrooms that helps you understand how the mushroom was able to grow so big, put that information in what you write, too.

_____

_____

_____

_____

Apply Read the sentences below. Then use what they tell you to draw a conclusion.

- The classes at the town's dance school are always full.

- Many people watch when the dance students perform.

- Most children in the town say they want to study dance.

- The dance school is moving to a bigger building next year.

Conclusion _____

_____

_____

Plurals of Words Ending in -y

Focus To make the plural form of a noun that ends with a -y that comes after a consonant, you change the y to i and add es. To make the plural of a noun that ends with -y that follows a vowel, you just add s.

Nouns that end with -y that follows a consonant:

      cherry   cherries   fly flies

Nouns that end in -y that follows a vowel:

      boy   boys   play   plays

Practice Look at the singular and plural nouns below. Underline the correct spelling for each plural noun.

1. butterfly   butterflys   butterflies

2. city   cities   citys

3. turkey   turkeys   turkies

4. story   storys   stories

5. day   daies   days

6. toy   toys   toies

Apply Make each of the nouns below plural.
Then use each plural noun in a sentence.

1. valley _____

_____

_____

2. penny _____

_____

_____

3. daisy _____

_____

_____

4. library _____

_____

_____

5. journey _____

_____

_____

Name _____   Date _____

Comparatives

Focus An adjective is used to describe a person, place, or thing. An adverb describes an action. Writers use both to make comparisons.

> Add the ending *-er* to adjectives and to some adverbs to compare two things.
>
> I am **short**. My brother is **shorter** than I am.
>
> Ron ran **fast**. Jeff ran **faster** than Ron.

Identify Look through selections that you have read to find examples of sentences that contain comparatives. Write one example on the lines below.

_____

_____

_____

_____

Practice Read the adjective or adverb next to each sentence. Add *-er* to make the adjective or adverb a comparative. Use it to complete each sentence.

1. small   That class is _____ than ours.

2. tall   This girl is _____ than her friend.

3. big   He took a _____ helping than she did.

4. slow   Jane is walking _____ than a snail.

5. hard   Anna works _____ this year than she did last year.

6. crazy   Your idea sounds _____ than my idea.

Apply Write sentences with the following words. Use comparatives to compare the words.

1. Alicia   Mary _____

_____

2. trucks   cars _____

_____

3. apples   bananas _____

_____

Sequence

Focus Sequence is the order in which things happen in a story. The more you know about when things happen in a story, the better you can understand the story.

Some sequence clue words tell

- the **order** in which things happen
  first, then, finally

- the **time** or when things happen
  tonight, in the morning, once upon a time

Identify Look through "The Elves and the Shoemaker" for examples of sequence words.

1. Underline the kind of sequence words the writer uses most often

   - time

   - order

2. List four examples.

   _____

   _____

   _____

   _____

Practice and Apply Write a story to go with
the pictures. Use sequence words to tell the time
and order of your story.

_____

_____

_____

_____

_____

_____

_____

_____

_____

Name _____ Date _____

Irregular Plurals

Focus Many nouns can be made plural by adding -*s*. Some nouns are spelled differently in the plural form.

An **irregular plural** is a noun that is spelled differently in the plural form.

child	⟶	children
goose	⟶	geese
ox	⟶	oxen

Practice and Apply Look at the words below. Circle the nouns that are spelled differently in the plural form. On the next page, write the plural for each word you circled. Then write a sentence using each of these words.

tooth	shoe	man	coat
coin	foot	tree	child
ox	mouse	train	gift

1. _____

_____

_____

2. _____

_____

_____

3. _____

_____

_____

4. _____

_____

_____

5. _____

_____

_____

6. _____

_____

_____

Superlatives

Focus Writers use adjectives and adverbs to make comparisons. When they compare more than two things, they use adjectives and adverbs called superlatives.

A superlative is

- usually formed by adding *-est*.
  hard<u>est</u>   young<u>est</u>

- used only to describe three or more things.
  John is the taller of the twins, but Bill is the <u>tallest</u> of the three brothers.

Change the spelling before adding *-est* to

- two-syllable words that end in *y*. Change the *y* to *i*.
  earl<u>y</u>   earl<u>i</u><u>est</u>

- words ending in a vowel and a consonant. Double the consonant.
  h<u>ot</u>   ho<u>tt</u>est

Practice Underline the superlatives in the following paragraph.

I just finished the silliest book, about a dog named Joe. He wanted to be the smartest dog ever. He tried to be the fastest by running around the biggest park. Then he decided to be the funniest by doing tricks.

Superlatives *(continued)*

Add *-est* to these adjectives to make them into superlatives. Match them with their sentences.

high cold fast old late

1. Last winter was the _____ that I can remember.

2. Suzanne is the _____ runner in her class.

3. What is the _____ mountain in the world?

4. The _____ monster movie is really scary.

5. My grandmother is the _____ member of my family.

Apply Write a sentence that uses each superlative word.

1. strongest _____

_____

2. longest _____

_____

Types of Sentences

Focus Writers use different kinds of sentences to make stories interesting.

- A sentence that tells is called a *statement*. It ends with a period.
    The elephant danced at the circus.

- A sentence that asks something is a *question*. It ends with a question mark.
    Will you go to the circus with me?

- A sentence that shows strong feelings ends with an exclamation mark.
    I'm so excited to see the clowns!

- A sentence that gives an order ends with a period or exclamation mark.
    Set the table.

Identify Look through "The Elves and the Shoemaker." Try to find an example of two kinds of sentences.

Sentence: _____

_____

Sentence: _____

_____

Practice and Apply Look at the picture.
Follow the directions to write sentences to go
with the picture.

1. Write a sentence that tells.

_____

2. Write a sentence that asks a question.

_____

3. Write a sentence that shows strong feeling.

_____

4. Write a sentence that orders.

_____

Name _____   Date _____

Cause and Effect

Focus In a story, one thing causes another thing to happen. Looking for causes and effects helps you to better understand story events.

> - A **cause** is why something happens.
> - An **effect** is what happens.
>   Because of the snow, school was closed.
>   ↑   ↑
>   cause   effect

Identify Look through "The Paper Crane" for something that makes something else happen. In the spaces below, write the cause and effect. Also write the pages where you find them.

1. Page: _____

   Cause: _____

   _____

2. Page: _____

   Effect: _____

   _____

Practice Read each sentence. Write the *effect* (what happened) and the *cause* (why it happened) for each sentence.

1. The eggs cracked because I dropped them on the floor.

   Effect: _____

   Cause: _____

2. The car won't start because Dad is using the wrong key.

   Effect: _____

   Cause: _____

3. The zipper was stuck, so I couldn't close my jacket.

   Effect: _____

   Cause: _____

Apply Think about what happened today. Write down one thing that happened—the effect. Then write why it happened—the cause.

Effect: _____

Cause: _____

Long Vowel Spelling Patterns

Focus Knowing that words or syllables that end in a silent *e* most often have a long vowel sound can help you improve your spelling.

Short Vowel Words	Long Vowel Words
mop	mope
scar	scare
slim	slime
cut	cute

Identify Find words in "The Paper Crane" or another story that have a long vowel and a silent *e* at the end. Write the words. Then use each word in a sentence.

1. _____

_____

_____

2. _____

_____

_____

Practice and Apply Look at the pairs of words below. Choose the word that completes the sentences and write that word in the blank.

1. The lion's _____ was long and thick.

        (man, mane)

2. I _____ I pass my test today.

      (hop, hope)

3. I _____ my bear when I sleep.

      (hug, huge)

4. Jim _____ spell anything.

      (can, cane)

5. Did you _____ your bike to school today?

      (rid, ride)

6. You must have a _____ if you are going to the doctor.   (not, note)

Synonyms

Focus Using the same word over and over can be boring. Writers use synonyms to make their writing more interesting and to say exactly what they mean.

> A synonym is a word that has the same or almost the same meaning as another word.
>
> | | |
> |---|---|
> | big | huge |
> | quiet | silent |

Practice Read each passage below. Then rewrite the passages, replacing the underlined words with words that mean almost the same, but are more interesting and descriptive.

1. Anna had a big dog. He lived in a big house. He had a big bark.

   _____

   _____

   _____

   _____

   _____

2. The book I am reading is <u>nice</u>. It has <u>nice</u> characters. It has a <u>nice</u> story.

_____

_____

_____

_____

_____

Apply Write a short paragraph describing a character from a favorite story that you have read. Then read the paragraph carefully. Look for words you can replace with more interesting or descriptive words.

_____

_____

_____

_____

_____

_____

_____

Name _____   Date _____

Telling About What Happened Before

(Irregular Past Tense)

Focus When something is already done, it is in the past. Verbs can tell about the past. Many verbs that show what happened end with *-ed*. For example, *own* and *owned*. Other verbs do not.

Some verbs show past tense by changing their spelling:

Present	**Past**
stand	stood

Practice Read each pair of sentences below. Read the past-tense verbs under each blank. Choose the correct one. Write it on the line.

1. Today I buy paper. Yesterday I _____ paper.   (buyed, bought)

2. Now birds fly. Last week they _____.
                                   (flied, flew)

3. Today I will make a paper crane.

   Yesterday I _____ a paper crane.
                  (maked, made)

4. Right now I see the sun.

An hour ago, I only _____ clouds.
(seed, saw)

5. Today I will begin a new book.

Yesterday I _____ a new book.
(beginned, began)

Apply Write a paragraph about something that happened at school yesterday or last week. Use the correct past-tense verbs.

_____

_____

_____

_____

_____

_____

_____

_____

_____

Following Clues
(Making Inferences)

Focus Instead of telling you everything,
writers sometimes just give you clues.

Information in a story gives the reader a clue.
Clues can help you know more about things
that happen in a story. Read this sentence:

> *John stood up and brushed off his
> clothing.*

The clue *stood up* tells you that John had
either fallen or was knocked down. The clue
brushed off tells you that his clothing got dirty.

Practice Read each sentence below. Write clues
from the sentence that tell what happened. Then
write what that clue tells you.

1. Lin was out of breath as she told the teacher
   about finding someone's glasses on the playground.

   Clue: _____

   What the clue tells you: _____

   _____

2. Jacob covered his ears when he heard his brother's music playing.

Clue: _____

What the clue tells you: _____

_____

Apply Look at the picture below. Write a paragraph about the picture without telling what the event is. Let your readers use the clues in your writing.

_____

_____

_____

_____

Suspense and Surprise

Focus Writers use suspense and surprise to make their stories more interesting.

- **Suspense** makes the reader want to find out what happens next.
- **Surprise** is when what happens next is not what the reader expected.

Identify Look through selections you have read in this unit. Find and write a passage that shows suspense or surprise.

_____

_____

_____

_____

_____

_____

_____

_____

Practice and Apply Write a paragraph about
an ordinary afternoon. Give it a surprise ending.
Begin with an afternoon at the library, a morning
on the playground, or helping at home. Plan an
unexpected, surprise ending.

_____

_____

_____

_____

_____

_____

_____

_____

_____

_____

_____

_____

_____

Final *e* with Endings
-*ed* and -*ing*

Focus When you add the -*ed* or -*ing* ending to words that end in *e*, you must drop the final *e*.

Words that end in *e*		
bake	baked	baking
phone	phoned	phoning
glide	glided	gliding

Identify Look through this story for words that end in -*ed* or -*ing*. Write the base word on the right and the word with the -*ed* or -*ing* ending on the left.

Word with Ending	Base Word
_____	_____
_____	_____
_____	_____
_____	_____
_____	_____
_____	_____

Practice Add *-ed* and *-ing* to each of the following verbs.

Verb	Add *-ed*	Add *-ing*
1. smile	_____	_____
2. move	_____	_____
3. paste	_____	_____
4. bounce	_____	_____
5. love	_____	_____

Apply Choose either the *-ed* or *-ing* ending of each of the verbs above. Use it in a sentence.

1. _____

_____

2. _____

_____

3. _____

_____

4. _____

_____

5. _____

_____

Context Clues

Focus As they read, readers sometimes come across words they do not know.

> One way readers can figure out the meaning of a word they don't know is to read the rest of the sentence or paragraph, called the *context* in which the word appears.
> Read the sentence *Plankton, tiny plant or animal life, weakly floats near the surface of the water.* You can figure out what *plankton* means from the words *tiny plant or animal life.*

Identify Look through "The Story of the Three Whales" for examples of difficult words that are explained with context clues. Write one example on the lines below.

_____

_____

_____

_____

_____

_____

Practice Read each sentence below. Write a definition for each underlined word. Use context clues to help you.

1. Gray whales can hold their breath under water for half an hour, but after that time they must <u>surface</u>.

   Definition: _____

   _____

   _____

2. A wall of ice had formed at the <u>mouth</u> of the bay so the whales could no longer swim out to sea.

   Definition: _____

   _____

   _____

Apply Write a sentence in which you use a difficult word. Write the sentence so that readers can figure out what the word means by reading it.

_____

_____

_____

_____

Pronouns

Focus Pronouns take the place of nouns. Using the correct pronoun makes your meaning clear.

A **pronoun** always refers to a **noun**.

> *John* dropped *his* book on the floor.

Some common pronouns are:

I	you	he	she
it	they	them	us
we	me	him	my
your	their	his	her

Practice Underline the pronoun in each sentence. Circle the noun the pronoun refers to.

1. Sue gave her sister a present.

2. The birds flew out of their nest.

3. Carlos wrote to Aunt Gloria after she moved.

4. Bill and I went to his house after school.

5. Maria and Fred are playing with her toys.

6. The cats were so happy they purred.

Practice Complete each sentence with one or more nouns.

7. _____ went to the movies with her sister.

8. Please give _____ his book.

9. _____ are playing a game with their marbles.

10. The mother _____ found some food for her babies.

Apply Write four sentences with nouns and pronouns in them.

1. Sentence with a noun and the pronoun *her*

   _____

2. Sentence with a noun and the pronoun *him*

   _____

3. Sentence with a noun and the pronoun *they*

   _____

4. Sentence with a noun and the pronoun *we*

   _____

Compare and Contrast

Focus Writers sometimes use **comparison and contrast** in a story to make an idea clearer and to make the story more interesting for the reader.

- **To compare** means to tell how things, events, or characters are alike.

- **To contrast** means to tell how things, events, or characters are different.

Identify Look through "The Whales' Song" for what Lilly's grandmother and great-uncle think about whales. In the spaces below write how their ideas are different. Then write how they are the same.

How their ideas are different:

_____

_____

_____

How their ideas are same:

_____

_____

_____

Practice Complete the sentence below. Then explain how it is alike and how it is different.

A pencil is like a _____ .

How are they alike? _____

_____

How are they different? _____

_____

Apply Write a sentence comparing two things. Then explain how they are alike and how they are different.

_____

_____

_____

How are they alike? _____

_____

_____

How are they different? _____

_____

_____

Fact and Opinion

Focus A story can include both facts and opinions about things or people. Story characters can have opinions, too.

- A **fact** can be checked and proven to be true.

- An **opinion** cannot be proven. It is one person's idea.

Identify Look in "The Whales' Song" to find some facts and opinions. Write a sentence that tells a *fact* about whales. Then write a sentence that tells Uncle Frederick's *opinion* about Lilly's grandmother's story.

1. Page: _____

Sentence that tells a fact about whales:

_____

_____

2. Page: _____

Sentence that tells Uncle Frederick's opinion about Lilly's grandmother's story:

_____

_____

Practice and Apply Read each topic. Then write one sentence that tells a fact and one sentence that tells an opinion about each topic.

1. Topic: School

Fact: _____

_____

Opinion: _____

_____

2. Topic: Basketball

Fact: _____

_____

Opinion: _____

_____

3. Topic: Friends

Fact: _____

_____

Opinion: _____

_____

Name _____ Date _____

Time and Order Words

Focus Knowing the time that things happen
in a story and the order in which they happen
helps you understand the story.

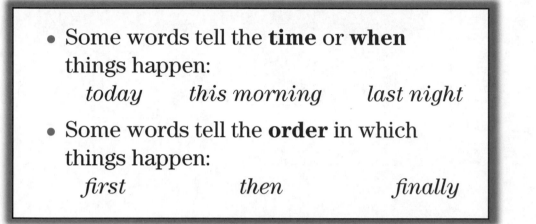

- Some words tell the **time** or **when**
  things happen:
  today   *this morning*   *last night*
- Some words tell the **order** in which
  things happen:
  first   *then*   *finally*

Identify Look through "The Whales' Song" to find
time and order words. List two examples of each.

Time Words

_____

_____

Order Words

_____

_____

Practice and Apply Write a story to go with the pictures. Use words that tell time and order in your story.

today
first
then

_____

_____

_____

_____

_____

_____

_____

_____

_____

_____

Possessive Nouns

Focus Use a possessive noun to show that something belongs to something else.

- Add apostrophe *s* (*'s*) to most singular nouns to show that they belong to something else.
- Add just an apostrophe (') to plural nouns that end in *s*.

Practice Write the possessive noun that goes with each phrase.

1. the uncle of the girl _____

2. the father of the twins _____

3. the string on the kite _____

4. the petals on the flowers _____

Write what each possessive noun means.

5. the book's cover _____

6. the cousins' friends _____

7. the sun's warmth _____

8. the sheep's wool _____

Apply Rewrite the sentences using possessive nouns.

1. The grandmother of Lilly told her a story.

   _____

   _____

2. The song of the whales is not a folktale.

   _____

   _____

3. The meat, bones, and blubber of a whale were useful.

   _____

   _____

4. The flower that belonged to Lilly danced on the waves.

   _____

   _____

Plot

Focus In a story, the plot is made up of the things that happen in the story.

> The **plot** of a story
>
> - usually starts with the **main characters**, the **setting**, and a **problem** to solve.
>
> - usually ends with a **climax** or high point of the story and a **solution** to the problem.

Identify Look in "Cinderella" for the main characters, the setting, and the problem in the story. Then list the main characters, setting, and problem below.

Main characters:

_____

_____

Setting:

_____

_____

Problem:

_____

Plot *(continued)*

Practice and Apply Choose another fairy tale
you know. Write the answers to the questions
about the plot in your own words.

Story title: _____

Main characters: _____

  1. Settings: Where and when does the story take place?

  _____

  _____

  2. Problem: What is the problem in the story?

  _____

  _____

  3. Main event: What is the climax or high point?

  _____

  _____

  _____

  4. End of story: How is the problem solved?

  _____

  _____

  _____

Name _____   Date _____

Multiple-Meaning Words

Focus Some words can confuse us because they have more than one meaning.

To tell which meaning is meant:

- Look at the rest of the sentence.

- Decide which meaning of the word makes the most sense in the sentence.

Here are examples of multiple meaning:
Please be *patient* while we wait for the bus.
He was the doctor's first *patient* today.

Identify Read through "Cinderella." Find examples of words that have more than one meaning. Write your results below.

1. Word _____   Page number _____

The word means: _____

2. Word _____   Page number _____

The word means: _____

3. Word _____   Page number _____

The word means: _____

Practice Look at the underlined word in each
sentence. Circle the meaning of the word that
fits the sentence best.

1. Our dog needed a <u>pen</u>.

   fenced-in place   writing tool

2. Sometimes the children argued over the <u>ball</u>.

   round toy that bounces   a formal dance

3. On her birthday, Julie wanted a new <u>band</u>
   for her hair.

   musicians   thin strip of ribbon

Apply Write two sentences for each of the
following words. Use a different meaning in each.

1. pound _____

   _____

   _____

2. wave _____

   _____

   _____

Point of View

Focus Point of view is the way in which a writer tells a story.

A story may be told from the **first-person point of view**.

- The person telling the story is also a character in the story.
- The clue words *I, we, me, my* are used. Example: *I ran into the hall to find out what happened!*

A story may be told from the **third-person point of view**.

- The person telling the story is not a character in the story.
- The clue words *he, she,* and *they* are used. Example: *They ran into the hall to find out why he was yelling.*

Identify Look in a favorite story for clue words that show who's telling the story. Write the clue words. Then tell whether the story is told from the first-person or the third-person point of view.

Clue Words: _____

From which point of view is the story told?

_____

_____

Practice Read each sentence. Fill in the circle next to the correct answer. Then underline the clue word in each sentence.

1. Early one morning, a beautiful butterfly appeared at my window.

   ○   first-person point of view

   ○   third-person point of view

2. She looked out the window.

   ○   first-person point of view

   ○   third-person point of view

3. Chris and I belong to the same club.

   ○   first-person point of view

   ○   third-person point of view

Apply Write one sentence from the third-person point of view.

1. _____

   _____

   _____

Write one sentence from the first-person point of view.

2. _____

   _____

   _____

Consonant Blends

Focus Sometimes two consonant letters stand for separate sounds that are blended together.

Knowing some of the common consonant blends will help you spell correctly.

Blend	Example
bl	block
cl	clamp
fl	flag
fr	frame
sn	snow
st	step

Practice Read each sentence. Using the box above, figure out what word goes in the sentence. Write in the letters that complete each word.

1. It is best to ___ ___ay inside when it is storming.

2. The water was so ___ ___ear I could see to the bottom of the pond.

3. Wild animals use camouflage to ___ ___end in.

4. The car had a ___ ___at tire in the back.

5. Animals that live in ___ ___owy areas are often white.

Make words by matching each blend with an ending. Then write each word you made.

6. sn   own   _____

7. tr   out   _____

8. br   ap   _____

9. str   eam   _____

Apply Find words in stories that you have read that begin with each blend below. Write the words under the blends. Then use three of the words in sentences.

st-	**cl-**	**br-**
_____	_____	_____
_____	_____	_____

1. _____

_____

2. _____

_____

3. _____

_____

Name _____ Date _____

Prefixes

Focus Recognizing prefixes helps you learn new words and understand their meanings.

A prefix is a syllable added to the beginning of a base word that changes the meaning of the base word.

Prefix	Meaning	Base Word	Example	Meaning
un-	not	fair	unfair	not fair
re-	again	paint	repaint	paint again
dis-	not	agree	disagree	not agree

Practice Circle the word in each sentence that has a prefix. What does the word mean? Write its meaning on the line.

1. Shelly is unhappy. _____

2. Let me recheck the answers. _____

3. Mark will refill the pitcher. _____

4. Ana is unsure about going to the park.

_____

5. Doug disagrees with me. _____

Apply Read the word in front of each sentence. Add
a prefix to that word and write it in the sentence.

1. set   We had to _____ our clocks
            after the power came back on.

2. plug   You should _____ the
            computer during a thunderstorm.

3. pack   Please _____ your suitcase
            and put your clothes away.

4. plant   We need to _____ the garden
            where the rain washed away the seeds.

5. write   _____ this paper so that I
            can read it.

6. appear   Did the magician really make

            her _____?

7. even   The table wobbled because the

            legs were _____.

8. healthy   Eating only junk food is

            _____.

9. tell   I can _____ that fairy tale in
            my own words.

Subject-Verb Agreement

Focus Every sentence must have a subject and a verb. The subject of a sentence can be singular or plural. The subject and verb must match.

To match subjects with **present tense** verbs:

- **Singular** subject—add *-s* to the verb
  The whale __lives__ in the ocean.

- **Plural** subject—don't change the verb
  Whales __live__ in the ocean.

Practice Underline the subject. Circle the verb. Write singular or plural on the line.

1. One animal looks for a place to hide. _____

2. Many animals look for a place to hide. _____

3. The birds build a nest. _____

4. The bird builds a nest. _____

5. The boy plays soccer. _____

6. The boys play soccer. _____

Subject-Verb Agreement *(continued)*

Apply Underline the correct verb to complete each sentence.

1. The baby deer (wait, waits) for its mother to return.

2. The bats (hang, hangs) by their feet.

3. Moles (dig, digs) tunnels.

4. A beaver (swim, swims) very well.

5. The young bullfrog (hop, hops) from log to log.

6. Tadpoles (grow, grows) into frogs.

Finish each sentence with a verb in the present tense. Be sure your verb matches with the noun.

7. Baby owls _____

_____

8. The mother fox _____

_____

9. The old raccoon _____

_____

10. Butterflies _____

_____

Main Idea

Focus The **main idea** tells what a paragraph is mostly about.

- A **main-idea sentence** gives the main idea of a paragraph. The other sentences in a paragraph give details or information about the main idea.

- A main-idea sentence often comes **first** in a paragraph. Placing the main idea sentence first helps readers know what the paragraph is about.

Identify Look through "Animal Camouflage" for main-idea sentences. Write one main-idea sentence below. Then give some details about the main idea.

Page: _____

Main idea: _____

_____

Details about the main idea: _____

_____

_____

Practice Read the paragraph. It is missing a main-idea sentence. Choose the correct main-idea sentence from the box and write it on the lines.

Parents tell their children stories about their childhoods. Grandparents talk about their lives and their parents' lives. When we learn our family's stories, we can tell our children the stories too.

Storytellers entertain many people.

Parents should talk to their children.

Families have picnics together.

Stories help bring families together.

_____

_____

Apply Add your own sentence to the paragraph above. It should give more information about the main idea.

_____

_____

_____

_____

Types of Sentences

Focus Writers use different kinds of
sentences to make stories more interesting.

Sentence Types

- A sentence that **tells** ends with a *period.*
  A snake slid under a rock.

- A sentence that **asks** ends with a
  question mark.
  Did you see that snake?

- A sentence that **shows strong feeling**
  ends with an *exclamation point.*
  Don't step on that snake!

Practice Put the correct mark at the end of
each sentence.

1. The frog jumped from the pond___

2. Can a toad jump___

3. That toad jumped really high___

4. How high did that toad jump___

Apply Use your own words to write different sentence types.

1. Sentence that **tells:**

_____

_____

_____

2. Sentence that **asks:**

_____

_____

_____

3. Sentence that **shows strong feeling:**

_____

_____

_____

Cause and Effect

Focus **Cause** and **effect** is when one thing causes another thing to happen. Looking for causes and effects can help you understand what you read.

> - The **cause** is why something happens.
> - The **effect** is what happens.

Identify Look in "What Color Is Camouflage?" for the effects listed below. Then write the cause for each effect.

1. Effect: Sticks seem to crawl, leaves can fly, and a stone may have eyes and a beak.

   Cause: _____

   _____

   _____

2. Effect: Chameleons, squids, and octopuses change colors to match their surroundings.

   Cause: _____

   _____

   _____

Practice Read each sentence. Write the effect (what happened) and the cause (why it happened).

1. Because it was hot, my friends went swimming.

   Effect: _____

   Cause: _____

2. Amy ran so fast that she won the race.

   Effect: _____

   Cause: _____

3. Since we wanted to be helpful, we picked up our toys.

   Effect: _____

   Cause: _____

Apply Write a sentence of your own that shows a cause and an effect. Draw a line under the cause in your sentence.

_____

_____

_____

_____

Suffixes

Focus Recognizing suffixes helps you learn new words and understand their meanings.

- A suffix comes after a base word.

Suffix	Meaning	Example	Meaning
-ful	full of	thankful	full of thanks
-less	without	careless	without care
-er	one who does	builder	one who builds
-ment	act of	enjoyment	act of enjoying
-ly	in a way that is	slowly	in a way that is slow

Practice Circle the word in each sentence that has a suffix. What does the word mean? Write its meaning on the line.

1. Shelly quickly walked to school.

_____

2. Renee is always cheerful.

_____

3. The farmer is plowing.

_____

4. The fearless superhero saved the day.

_____

Apply Read the word in front of each sentence. Add a suffix to that word and write it in the sentence.

1. quick   The car stopped _____.

2. fear   Pat was _____ that her
dog was lost.

3. agree   Are we in _____ about
our plans?

4. care   _____ people often get hurt.

5. teach   Mrs. Henry is the best _____
in the school.

6. thank   We were _____ that
we got home safely.

Adverbs

Focus Adverbs are words that tell more about verbs. Adverbs describe the action in a sentence.

- **Adverbs** usually tell *when, where,* or *how.*
  The dog ran *away.*

- Many adverbs end in *-ly.*
  Carol ate her breakfast *quickly.*

Practice Read each sentence. Write the adverb on the line. Then write if the adverb tells *when, where,* or *how.*

1. We walk quickly down the street. _____

2. The birds fly high above our heads. _____

3. I will return soon. _____

4. Ann lives far across town. _____

5. She ran fast. _____

6. We will eat lunch early today. _____

Underline the adverb in each sentence. What question does the adverb answer? Write the answer on the line.

7. Our family eats breakfast early. _____

8. The children boarded the bus quietly. _____

9. The ducks swam away. _____

Write an adverb to complete the sentences.

10. The deer ran _____.

11. The lions roared _____.

12. The cat purred _____.

13. The pigs squealed _____.

Apply Write one sentence about something that happened at school. Use one adverb. Underline the adverb.

_____

_____

_____

_____

Drawing Conclusions

Focus Thinking about the information in a
story can help readers make decisions about
what is happening.

> Readers can **draw conclusions** about a
> character or event in a story by using
> information in the story's words and pictures.
> With this information, a reader can make a
> statement about a character or event. A
> conclusion must be supported by the
> information in the story.

Identify Read these sentences from "They Thought
They Saw Him." Write the conclusion you can make
from the underlined information in each sentence.

1. <u>All winter</u> little dark chameleon had lived,
   <u>safe and asleep</u>, beneath the granary where
   the people kept their seed corn.

   _____

   _____

2. As he moved on <u>quick silent feet</u>, he began
   to forget the sleepy winter dark and felt
   the joy in the first <u>wakeful light of spring</u>.

   _____

   _____

Practice and Apply Read the following
paragraph. Then answer the questions below
by drawing conclusions.

     Our teacher, Ms. Smith, began talking to
herself. "Now, where are they? I can't read
without them." She looked through her desk
drawers. She looked in her purse. She patted
her pockets. As Ms. Smith scratched her head,
we began to giggle. She found what she had
been looking for. "I always leave them up
there," she laughed.

What was Ms. Smith doing?

_____

_____

Why did the students giggle when
Ms. Smith scratched her head?

_____

_____

Special Spelling Patterns: /aw/ Sound

Focus All of the words in this lesson have the /aw/ sound.

All of these words have the /aw/ sound.			
ough	**augh**	**all**	**alk**
thought	daughter	ball	walk
bought	caught	mall	talk

Practice

fought	taught	call	tall	talk

Use the words in the box to complete the sentences.

1. There is a telephone _____ for you.

2. That basketball player is very _____.

3. Shh! Please don't _____ during the movie.

4. Everyone in our school is _____ to use a computer.

5. The man _____ a bear in the mountains.

mall walk thought bought daughter

Use the words in the box to complete the sentences.

6. Meet us at the ice cream shop in the _____.

7. The class took a _____ around the block.

8. Sam _____ that he would play basketball after school.

9. Debbie _____ cupcakes on her birthday.

10. His _____ was coming home for a visit.

Apply Write two sentences. Use a word with the /aw/ sound.

1. _____

_____

2. _____

_____

High-Frequency Words

Focus Many of the words that we use often do not follow the rules. These words have to be learned by sight.

Some **high-frequency words** cannot be sounded out and spelled, using the sounds and spellings that we have learned.

was	**again**	**their**

Practice Read each high-frequency word in the box below. Use the words to complete the sentence.

this	enough	many	says	these	your

1. My mother _____ she wants us home by dark.

2. _____ books must belong to Sarah or Jack.

3. Is _____ Tom's coat on the floor?

4. Are _____ boots in the closet?

5. _____ of the swings are broken.

6. Have you had _____ to eat?

Apply Write sentences using the high-frequency words below.

friend	said	saw	every	none	where

1. _____

_____

2. _____

_____

3. _____

_____

4. _____

_____

5. _____

_____

6. _____

_____

Classify and Categorize

Focus **Classifying and categorizing** means putting things into groups. Classifying can help readers keep track of information in a story.

To classify information,

- name the categories for things, characters, or events

- list the things, characters, or events that fit under each category

- Sometimes things, characters, or events can fit into more than one category.

  pencil   pen   paper   folder   glue

  School supplies   **Writing instruments**

  pen, pencil, glue   pen, pencil
  paper, folder

Identify The characters in *How the Guinea Fowl Got Her Spots* can be classified in a number of different ways. Look at the categories listed below and write the animals that fit under each.

Friends: _____

Large animals: _____

Small animals: _____

Four-legged animals: _____

Practice Look at the list of things below. List each thing under the correct category. Remember, some things can fit in more than one category.

pencil	cutting board	scissors	chalkboard
sponge	eraser	paper	can opener

**Things that are useful
in a school classroom**

**Things that are
useful in a kitchen**

_____   _____

_____   _____

_____   _____

_____   _____

_____   _____

Apply Make a list of other things that would fit into each of the categories above.

School classroom: _____

_____

Kitchen: _____

_____

Frequently Misspelled Words

Focus Sometimes, the wrong spelling can give your reader the wrong idea!

Here are a few commonly misspelled words:

- its   *The dog bit its tail.*
- it's   *It's Monday morning.*
- past   *In the past, she was an excellent swimmer.*
- passed   *I passed your house yesterday.*
- than (comparative)
              Bradley is taller than Barbara.
- then   *Then he said, "Why don't you come with us?"*

Practice Underline the misspelled words in the following sentences.

1. Than the ogre started walking toward the children.

2. I past my math test!

3. Its time to go home.

Apply Here are some more commonly misspelled words:

your, you're	won, one	no, know
quit, quite, quiet	sum, some	

If the underlined word is incorrect, cross it out and write the correct word above it. If the word is correct, don't change it!

Sum people I know are really silly. Once they start, its quite impossible to get them to stop. Donny, for example, is won of my best friends. But when he starts being silly, you feel like he's you're worst enemy. The other day he started singing, "I'm a soul man!" over and over. Than he started to pretend he was playing the guitar. I passed by him in the hallway and tried to ignore him. It's hard to no what to do when a good friend starts acting up.

Punctuating Dialogue

Focus Good writers use quotation marks to show the exact words of the speaker.

Quotation marks are used to show where each person's words start and end. That's why quotation marks go right before the first word spoken, and right after the last word spoken.

  "Did you have a good day at school, dear?" my mother asked me.

  I told her, "It was picture day and I forgot to wear my new shirt!"

Identify Look for sentences of dialogue in the selection, "How the Guinea Fowl Got Her Spots." Copy two lines of dialogue with the quotation marks correctly placed, on the lines below.

1. Page: _____

  Line: _____

  _____

2. Page: _____

  Line: _____

  _____

Practice Place quotation marks where they should go in the following story.

Do you ever wonder about anything? Mrs. Barnett asked her class.

Akusha raised her hand. I wonder why the sky is blue, she said.

I wonder if fish get thirsty, said Harley.

Anybody else? asked Mrs. Barnett.

I wonder something! Simon was waving his hand madly and the teacher called on him. He said, Can clamshells tap dance?

Everybody laughed, including Mrs. Barnett.

Apply Write a short paragraph about playing with a friend. Make sure to include dialogue with quotation marks.

_____

_____

_____

_____

_____

_____

_____

Verbs with -ed and -ing

Focus Some verbs double their final consonant before you add -ed or -ing to them.

- If the verb (or the last syllable of the verb) has a long vowel sound, use only one consonant at the end of the word.
  write → writing (drop the silent e before adding the ending)

- If the verb (or the last syllable of the verb) has a short vowel sound, double the final consonant.
  slam → slamming or slammed

Practice Decide whether the following words need to double their final consonants. Then add the suggested ending. Write the correct spelling on the line.

1. hop (ing) _____

2. share (ing) _____

3. plan (ed) _____

4. scare (ed) _____

5. hope (ing) _____

6. pet (ing) _____

Add to the list three words that need their final consonants doubled. Then write the word with an ending.

get _____   **getting** _____

_____   _____

_____   _____

Apply What was it like when you were learning to read? Who helped you? How did they help you? Write a paragraph about when you were learning to read. Pay special attention to words that end in *-ing* or *-ed*. Do they need the double consonant?

_____

_____

_____

_____

_____

_____

_____

Commas in a Series

Focus Commas are often used to separate words or phrases in a series of at least three things.

- Patty went to the store and bought apples, oranges, pears, and bananas.

- Tommy, Jeff, Jason, and Bobby saw the latest action movie together.

- The girls went ice skating, played basketball, rode bikes, and ate pizza.

Practice Look at the series of words or phrases in the following sentences. Decide where the commas go and add them.

1. My favorite ice cream flavors are chocolate pecan vanilla and pumpkin.

2. Last summer my family visited Detroit Chicago Seattle and San Francisco.

3. On our camping trip we went fishing hiking hunting swimming and diving.

4. Before you can drive a car you have to take a class read a book on driving rules take driving lessons and pass a test.

5. Martha Allen Samantha and Jill plan to do their homework eat dinner wash up and watch some TV.

Apply For each of the following categories, write a sentence using a series of three or more things. Use commas correctly. The first one is done for you.

1. vegetables   **The vegetables I hate the most are broccoli, peppers, and spinach.**

2. sports _____

_____

_____

3. friends _____

_____

_____

4. activities you do in the park _____

_____

_____

5. toys _____

_____

_____

Words Ending in -il, -al, or -le

Focus Words that end with the same sound can be spelled several different ways. If you are not sure which spelling to use, find the word in a dictionary or ask for help.

One way to learn the spelling of a word is to look at the word and picture it in your mind. Then remember how it is written.

- Some words have *il* in the last syllable: *pupil*, *pencil*.

- Other words have *al* in the last syllable: *equal*, *final*.

- Another group of words has *le* in the last syllable: *gentle*, *invisible*.

Practice Complete each word below with *il*, *al*, or *le*. Then write the word on the line. Use the box to help choose the correct ending.

---

pencil	animal	fossil	mammal
equal	juggle	vegetable	gentle

---

1. penc __ __ _____

3. vegetab __ __ _____

2. equ __ __ _____

4. foss __ __ _____

5. gent __ __ _____

7. jugg __ __ _____

6. mamm __ __ _____

8. anim __ __ _____

Apply In each sentence below, circle the word that is spelled wrong. Then, write the correct spelling on the line.

1. Samantha was an excellent puple. _____

2. In that cartoon, an anval is always falling on

someone's head. _____

3. The cattil looked happy, grazing in the field.

_____

4. Ann no longer had a fever. Her temperature

was normle. _____

5. To make himself visibil, the Invisible
Man wrapped himself in sheets.

_____

Abbreviations

Focus An abbreviation is a shorter way of writing a title, or word.

> • Abbreviations begin with a capital letter.
> • They end with a period.
>   Captain Miller ⟶ Capt. Miller

Practice Find the names and titles in each sentence below. Circle them. Then write them correctly on the line following the sentence.

1. Our teacher's name is mr Daly.

   _____

2. I help my next door neighbor mrs Reed after school.

   _____

3. I went to dr Myers for a checkup.

   _____

Apply Write three sentences. Use one abbreviation from the box in each sentence.

Mr.	Mrs.	Dr.

1. _____

_____

_____

2. _____

_____

_____

3. _____

_____

_____

Name _____ Date _____

Subjects and Predicates

Focus A sentence must have a subject and a predicate.

- The **subject** tells who or what.

- A **compound subject** has more than one subject. A compound subject often has the word **and**.
  The **dog and cat** *played*.

- The **predicate** tells what the subject is or does. A predicate always has a **verb**.

- A **compound predicate** has more than one verb.
  The cat **jumped and ran** away from the dog.

Practice Write a compound subject to complete each sentence.

1. The _____ played.

2. _____ got out of bed.

3. _____ were dancing.

4. _____ looked outside.

Write a compound verb to complete the predicate in each sentence.

5. Gary _____ a puppy.

Reading and Writing Workbook • *Compound Subjects and Predicates*   **147**

6. He _____ it home.

7. The puppy _____ some water.

8. It _____ with Gary's sister.

Read each sentence. Draw a line under the subject and circle the verb. If there is a compound subject or compound verb, underline or circle both parts.

9. James swam and walked at the park.

10. Squirrels and birds watched from a tree.

11. Fish swam and ate in the pond.

12. Sue and Carol went to the park.

Apply Write three sentences of your own. Underline the subject and circle the verb. Try to use a compound subject or compound predicate.

1. _____

_____

2. _____

_____

3. _____

_____

Compound Words

Focus A compound word is made up of two words put together.

> **Compound words** are made by putting together two words to create a new word.
>
> pop + corn = popcorn
> suit + case = suitcase
> basket + ball = basketball

Practice Identify and underline the compound words in the following sentences.

1. Marcy wants to be a firefighter when she grows up.

2. Has anyone seen Jose's backpack?

3. Last summer, my family visited a beautiful waterfall in the mountains.

4. Look how the lake sparkles in the moonlight!

5. It is important for children to play outside in the sunshine.

weed	foot	giving	thanks
sea	mark	book	ball

Apply Make compound words from the words above. Then write a sentence for each compound word.

1. _____

_____

2. _____

_____

3. _____

_____

4. _____

_____

Point of View

Focus **Point of view** is how the author decides to tell the story. He or she can tell it through a character or through someone outside of the story.

When a story is told from the **first-person point of view**

- the storyteller is a character in the story
- the clue words *I, my, mine, us, our,* and *we* are used

When a story is told from the **third-person point of view**

- the storyteller is not a character in the story
- the clue words *she, he, her, they,* and *their* are used

Identify Look in "Molly the Brave and Me" for clue words that show who is telling the story. Write the words and the name of the character telling the story.

Page: _____

Clue words: _____

_____

Who is telling the story? _____

Find an example in which the storyteller shares
her own thoughts or feelings. Write the first three
or four words of the example. Share your example
with your classmates.

Page: _____

Example: _____

_____

Practice Read the paragraphs. Circle each
word that gives a clue about the viewpoint that
the author uses to tell the story.

1. Marsha and her mother almost missed the
   plane. They had a hard time getting a taxi to
   the airport. Luckily, their plane was late taking off.

2. "That is my pencil," I said. "Please use the
   blue pencil instead of mine."

3. Jamie and I shared our snacks. Dad gave us
   apples, sandwiches, and peanuts. We ate
   the snacks at the picnic table.

Apply Write about something you and a friend
did together. Remember to use words such as *I,
me, my, we, us,* and *our.*

_____

_____

_____

Punctuation in a Letter

Focus It is important to use correct punctuation in letters. It shows the reader where to pause or stop.

> A comma goes after the greeting in a letter. A comma also follows the closing of a personal letter or note.

Practice Look at the three letters below. Add commas where they are needed.

1.

December 1, 2000

Dear Santa

    I have been a very good girl. Please bring me your best surprise.

    Fondly

    Aurora

2.

March 10, 1999

Dear Grandma

    My class is presenting a St. Patrick's Day play on March 17th at 2:00 p.m. I hope you can come!

    Love

    Jennifer

3.

July 4, 1999

Dear Lucy

    I have just arrived at camp. There are five other kids in my cabin. They seem nice. One guy is named Stewart. He says camp is really great, except for the food.

    Your friend

    John

Apply Many people work at your school. These workers may include the secretaries, librarians, custodians, crossing guards, teachers, principals, cooks, and bus drivers. On the lines below, write a letter to one of these workers. Thank the worker for the work they do. Be sure to add commas after the greeting and the closing.

_____

_____

_____

_____

_____

_____

_____

_____

Setting

Focus The setting is when and where a story takes place. Writers make a setting interesting for readers. They tell how the place looks, sounds, smells, or feels.

- The story may take place today, yesterday, or in the future. The setting may even be an exact time, such as "on Friday afternoon."

- The setting may be an imaginary place such as Never-Never Land. It may be a place such as Chicago. It may be an exact place like "the closet in my bedroom."

- A story may have more than one setting.

Practice Read each story beginning. Mark an X before the correct setting.

1. Joey ran onto the playground. His feet made tracks in the snow. He was ready to make a snowman.

   _____ This story takes place on the playground in winter.

   _____ This story takes place in a spaceship in the future.

   _____ This story takes place on a farm long ago.

2. Marissa loved her house. She could sit on the porch and see beautiful butterflies and birds. Summer was the best time of the year, Marissa thought.

_____ This story takes place on a boat in the ocean.

_____ This story takes place on Marissa's front porch in summer.

_____ This story takes place in a school classroom in winter.

Apply Read the story and answer the questions.

The Swimming Pool

Susie and Ron splashed each other every time they could. They loved being at the swimming pool. It was June, and school had just ended. The two friends were ready to play.

1. When did the story take place?

_____

_____

2. Where did the story take place?

_____

_____

Letter Patterns

Focus Knowing common letter patterns, or phonograms, and their pronunciation can help you read and spell many unfamiliar words.

- A phonogram is a letter pattern that has a vowel sound plus a consonant sound. A phonogram needs a beginning consonant to make it a word.

- Some common phonograms are

-at	-eak	-ide	-og	-ush
-ack	-ell	-ig	-ot	-ug
-ad	-ew	-ime	-ock	-un
-amp	-end	-ight	-od	-ut
-and	-ent	-ick	-op	-ub

Practice Look through "The Hole in the Dike" to find one word for each of the following phonograms.

    -and   -ell   -ick   -op

_____   _____   _____   _____

    -ug   -eak   -ush   -ew

_____   _____   _____   _____

Write four words for each of the
following phonograms:

1. -amp _____ _____ _____ _____

2. -end _____ _____ _____ _____

3. -ig _____ _____ _____ _____

4. -od _____ _____ _____ _____

5. -un _____ _____ _____ _____

Apply Choose some of the words you have
written to write three sentences on the lines below.

_____

_____

_____

_____

_____

_____

_____

Name _____ Date _____

Point of View

Focus A story's point of view explains who is telling the story.

- A story told from the first-person point of view is told by a character in the story. Clue words are *I, we, me, us, my, our.*

- Other stories are told by someone who is not in the story. These stories are told from the third-person point of view. Clue words are *he, she, them, they, his, her, theirs.*

Practice Read the sentences below and label each set as either first-person point of view or third-person point of view. Below each set, write the clue words for those sentences. The first one is done for you.

__First-person__ **1.** My dad calls me a long gulp of air. I think that's funny. We like to laugh together.

    my   me   I   we
   _____

_____ **2.** We traveled many miles to Indiana. My family was weary when we finally crossed the Ohio River.

   _____

_____ **3.** The family liked having a picnic, but they fussed about the ants. Don and his friends were late arriving.

_____

_____ **4.** Both girls wanted to read the book, but the librarian could give it to only one of them. They decided to read it as partners.

_____

Apply Write a sentence for each word listed below. In the first sentence, use the first-person point of view. In the second sentence, use third-person point of view.

   goose   **celebrate**

First-person point of view sentence:

_____

_____

Third-person point of view sentence:

_____

_____

Contractions

Focus Knowing how to make and use contractions can help you be a better writer.

- A **contraction** is one word made of two words put together. One or more letters are left out.

- An **apostrophe** takes the place of the missing letters.
  We are going to the lake.
  We're going to the lake.
  We + are = We're

- The words *will not* are special. To make the contraction, the letters change to make the word **won't**.

Practice Write the two words that make up each contraction.

1. aren't _____   _____

2. didn't _____   _____

Write the contraction formed by each pair of words.

3. do not _____

4. does not _____

Draw a line to match each pair of words to the correct contraction.

5. he is   he'll

6. he will   I've

7. I have   he's

8. I will   I'll

Apply Rewrite the sentence. Use a contraction in place of the underlined words.

1. Sea otters <u>are not</u> exactly the same as river otters.

_____

_____

Write two sentences of your own. Use a contraction in each sentence.

2. _____

_____

3. _____

_____

Prefixes and Suffixes

Focus Recognizing prefixes and suffixes in words helps you learn new words and understand their meanings.

> - A **prefix** is a syllable added to the beginning of a base word.
>
> - A **suffix** is a syllable added to the end of a base word.
>
> | Prefix | Meaning | Example |
> |--------|---------|---------|
> | un- | not | unfair |
> | re- | again | repaint |
> | dis- | not | disagree |
> | **Suffix** | **Meaning** | **Example** |
> | -ful | full of | helpful |
> | -less | without | careless |
> | -er | one who does | teacher |
> | -ly | in a way that is | quickly |

Practice Complete each sentence. Add one of the prefixes or suffixes from the box to the underlined word in the sentence. Write the new word.

1. If you are not <u>afraid</u>, you are _____.

2. If you <u>read</u> a story you have read before, you

   _____ the story.

3. A doll without <u>hair</u> is _____.

4. A kitten that likes to <u>play</u> is _____.

5. A person who <u>builds</u> is a _____.

6. If you are a <u>slow</u> walker, you walk _____.

7. If you do not <u>agree</u>, you _____.

Look at the word next to each sentence. Choose
a prefix or a suffix from the box on page 163
and add it to the word. Write the new word to
complete the sentence.

8. tied   Sue _____ her shoelaces
before taking off her shoes.

9. fear   Carl was _____ that his cat
had shredded his homework.

10. heat   We need to _____ the soup
because it has gotten cold.

Apply Add a suffix or a prefix to each word to
make two new words.

1. _____use   **2.** use_____

Now use each new word in a sentence.

3. _____

_____

4. _____

_____

Sequence

Focus A good writer leads readers through a story.

> Events in a story are told in a set order, or **sequence**. Following the sequence of events helps readers better understand a story.
>
> Looking for words that show time can help readers follow the sequence of events. Some examples of these words are: *first, then, later.*

Identify Think about or reread "The Empty Pot." Write down four things that happened in the story. Write them in the order they happened.

1. _____

   _____

2. _____

   _____

3. _____

   _____

4. _____

   _____

Practice Read this paragraph carefully. Then number the pictures in the correct sequence.

Seth gets up every morning at seven o'clock. Every morning he does the same things. He gets dressed first. Then he makes his bed. After that he brushes his teeth. About fifteen minutes later, Seth is ready for breakfast.

_____

_____

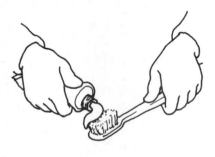

_____

_____

Apply Write sentences about something you know how to do, such as making a sandwich, brushing your teeth, or walking to school. Make sure the sequence of events is clear.

_____

_____

Verbs Ending with -ed and -ing

Focus Words can be changed by adding endings, such as -ed and -ing.

- The spelling of many words does not change when -ed or -ing is added.

  walk   walked   walking

- If a verb (or last syllable of the verb) has a short vowel sound, double the final consonant.

  slip   slipped   slipping

- If a verb ends with e, drop the e before adding -ed or -ing.

  hope   hoped   hoping

- If a verb ends with a consonant and y, change the y to i before adding -ed. Do not change it before adding -ing.

  cry   cried   crying

Practice Add -ed and -ing to each of the words below.

	-ed	-ing
1. rake	_____	_____
2. spy	_____	_____
3. look	_____	_____
4. pin	_____	_____

Verbs Ending with -ed and -ing *(continued)*

Complete each sentence by adding *-ed* or *-ing*
to each word under the blank.

5. The Emperor was _____ for

look

someone to take his place.

6. Ping _____ home with his seed.

hurry

7. Ping _____ he could get the seed to grow.

believe

8. All the children were _____ to show

run

the Emperor their flowers.

Apply Add *-ed* or *-ing* to the following words
and use the new words in sentences.

    carry   pass   hum   smile

1. _____

_____

2. _____

_____

3. _____

_____

4. _____

_____

Using Context Clues

Focus When we read, we sometimes find words we do not know. Often there are clues in the sentences that can help us figure out the meanings of words we don't know. These clues are context clues.

Kinds of Context Clues

- Definition

  For dinner we had *arroz con pollo*, which is Spanish for "chicken with rice."

- More Information

  The *island* was beautiful. The water surrounding it was crystal clear.

- Synonym

  Suzie's *valiant* grandfather, like other brave men, stood up for what he believed in.

- Antonym

  Bill didn't *submit* to the bully. He fought back.

Practice Read each sentence. Figure out the meaning of the underlined word. Then write the context clues that helped you.

1. The lady wore a <u>babushka</u>, or scarf, on her head.

_____

2. There were three ships docked at the <u>wharf</u>.

_____

3. That ring holds a <u>genuine</u>, not fake, jewel.

_____

4. The scientist studied <u>botany</u>. His plant studies were

famous. _____

5. That vase is <u>porcelain</u>. That fine, delicate china is valuable.

_____

Apply Choose two underlined words from above.
Write new sentences using the words correctly.

_____

_____

_____

_____

_____

_____

Author's Purpose

Focus Authors write for different reasons. Sometimes they want to give their readers information. Sometimes they want to entertain readers.

Writers *entertain* readers by including
- funny words and events
- exciting or familiar events

Writers *inform* readers by including
- facts that can be proven true

Writers *persuade* readers by including
- their opinions
- facts to support their opinions

Writers *explain* to readers how to do something by including
- the steps in a process

Identify Reread the part of "Brave As a Mountain Lion" that takes place at the spelling bee. Tell which part of this section shows the author's purpose.

Page: _____

Author's Purpose: _____

How did the author show the purpose? _____

_____

_____

_____

Practice Numbered below are some titles of stories. A list of purposes that authors can use is in the box. Choose the one that best fits each title.

entertain   inform   persuade   explain

1. "Why the School Year Should Be Longer"

_____

2. "Racing Through Outer Space"

_____

3. "The Great Mahooleywhazit and the Big YUCK!"

_____

4. "How to Feed a Baby"

_____

5. "Ocean Animals"

_____

Apply Choose one of the titles above and write the first sentence of the story.

_____

_____

_____

_____

Author's Purpose • **Reading and Writing Workbook**

Parts of Speech

Focus Language is made up of different kinds of words called **parts of speech**.

- A **noun** names a person, place, or thing.
  John rides the bus.
- A **pronoun** takes the place of a noun.
  He rides the bus.
- A **verb** names an action or tells what someone or something is, was, or will be.
  John rides the bus.
  John is a student.
- An **adjective** describes a noun or pronoun.
  He rides a yellow bus.
- An **adverb** describes a verb. It may answer the question *how? how often? when?* or *where?*
  John often rides the bus.

Practice Underline the word in each sentence that is the part of speech listed on the left.

1. adverb   A snail moves slowly across the sidewalk.

2. noun   The grasshopper jumped away.

3. adjective   An elephant has a long trunk.

Parts of Speech (*continued*)

4. verb   We painted the old gray barn.

5. pronoun   Ellen wore her hat.

Read the paragraph below. Find at least one word from the paragraph for each part of speech. Write each word in the correct place in the chart.

    Eve made the costumes for the school play. She worked quickly. The costumes looked beautiful.

noun	pronoun	verb	adjective	adverb

Apply Complete each sentence. Write a word that is the part of speech listed to the left.

1. adjective   It was a very _____ day.

2. verb   The scouts decided to _____ to the park.

3. adverb   They hiked _____ up the hill.

4. noun   At the top, they saw a _____.

5. pronoun   _____ was beautiful.

6. adjective   My cat has _____ eyes.

Long and Short Vowel Patterns: Review

Focus In a one-syllable word, that has a vowel-consonant-final *e* pattern, the vowel is long and the final *e* is silent.

Look at the following word pairs to see what the silent *e* does to the vowel.

mad	rip	rob	tub
made	ripe	robe	tube

When you see words with the silent *e* on the end, remember that the vowel sound in the middle usually is long.

Identify Look through "Immigrants: Coming to America" for examples of words with the silent *e*. Write them on the lines below.

1. _____

2. _____

3. _____

4. _____

Practice Circle the correct word in each sentence.

1. I gave my dog a (hug, huge).

2. The pear was juicy and (rip, ripe).

3. We (hop, hope) she can go with us.

4. Sally can (bit, bite) the apple.

5. Where is the roll of (tap, tape)?

6. An elephant weighs a (ton, tone)!

Apply Choose two words from the box. Use each word in a sentence.

rat	rate	fir	fire

1. _____

   _____

   _____

2. _____

   _____

   _____

Comparatives and Superlatives

Focus A common way to compare nouns is by adding *-er* or *-est* to the end of an adjective.

> When comparing two people, places, or things, add the ending *-er*. When comparing more than two people, places, or things, add the ending *-est*.
>
> *soft*　　　*softer*　　　*softest*

Identify Look through "Immigrants: Coming to America" for examples of *-er* and *-est* endings. Write words that have each ending on the lines below.

-er

_____

_____

_____

-est

_____

_____

_____

Practice Write a sentence that uses the given word.

1. older _____

_____

2. oldest _____

_____

3. stronger _____

_____

4. strongest _____

_____

Apply Describe and compare two parts of your home.

_____

_____

_____

_____

_____

_____

_____

Homophones and Homographs

Focus **Homophones** are words that sound alike but are spelled differently and have different meanings.

Here are some examples of homophones:

ate	eight	hear	here
see	sea	pair	pear
sale	sail	meat	meet
deer	dear		

Practice and Apply Draw a circle around the correct homophone to complete the sentence

1. We saw a (dear, deer) in the woods.

2. When you (hear, here) the bell, it is time to go.

3. A (pair, pear) is a kind of a fruit.

4. The (meet, meat) looked ready to eat.

5. There are (eight, ate) people in our family.

6. (Our, hour) bedtime is the same.

7. Did she (sea, see) the parade?

8. The shoe (sale, sail) was over yesterday.

Focus **Homographs** are words that are spelled
the same but have different meanings.

fair	date	batter

Practice and Apply Use a dictionary to help you
find homographs that complete each pair of
sentences. Write the meaning of each homograph.

1. What is the _____ of your birthday?

_____ means _____.

We eat _____ around the holiday.

_____ means _____.

2. Pour the _____ into the skillet.

_____ means _____

_____.

The _____ hit a home run.

_____ means _____.

3. It's not _____ that Jenny gets to stay up later.

_____ means _____.

I'm going to ride a pony at the _____.

_____ means _____.

Name _____ Date _____

Irregular Past Tense

Focus A **regular verb** has a past tense that ends in *-ed*. An **irregular verb** has a past tense that does not follow the *-ed* pattern.

Regular Verbs

Present Tense	Past Tense
walk	walked
stop	stopped

Irregular Verbs

Present Tense	Past Tense
give	gave
swim	swam
drink	drank

Identify Look through the story "Dreamplace" for examples of irregular verbs. Write the verbs on the lines below.

_____

_____

_____

_____

_____

_____

Practice Choose the correct spelling of the past tense verb to complete the sentence.

1. The gorilla (sat, sitted) in the cage.

2. The bee (stinged, stung) the girl.

3. Frank (getted, got) a new bicycle.

4. Sara (gave, gived) the teacher her report.

Apply Write the irregular verbs in the blanks below. The first one has been done for you.

Present Tense	Past Tense
drive	**drove**
take	
do	
go	
see	
say	
meet	
eat	

Name _____ Date _____

Frequently Misspelled Words

Focus Most words follow certain rules of spelling. However, some words can cause problems for even the best writers.

again	because	built	could
cousin	enough	every	first
here	house	lessons	letters
people	raise	read	remember
right	store	teacher	their
through	write	before	when
another			

Practice Circle the correct spelling of each word. Use a dictionary if you need help.

before	cuzzin	enough	peeple
befour	cousin	enuf	people

howse	built	write	raize
house	bilt	rite	raise

Circle the word that is misspelled in each sentence. Then write each misspelled word correctly.

1. We watch evry penny. _____

2. Many people gathered heer. _____

3. I learned all the ledders in a flash. _____

4. I culd not decide what I wanted to be when I grew up.

_____

5. Can we go to the movie agin? _____

6. My piano lesins are every Monday afternoon.

_____

7. Furst grade was a fun year for me. _____

8. You may not stay up, becuz it is your bedtime.

_____

9. Whin can I go to the park with you? _____

10. Mary saw anuther way to solve the problem.

_____

Apply Choose three words you sometimes misspell.
Write a sentence for each word.

1. _____

_____

2. _____

_____

3. _____

_____

Commas in a Series

Focus A comma follows each item in a series except the last one.

- Use commas to separate items in a series.

- Before the last item in a series, use either *and* or *or*.

- Make sure to use a comma before the word *and* or *or*.
    Will you have coffee, tea, or milk?
    Mrs. Alvarez, Mr. Lee, Mrs. Berg, and Dr. Johnson helped us.

Identify Read through "A Place Called Freedom." Find examples of items listed in a series. Look for the commas. Write your results below.

1. Page: _____

The series I found: _____

_____

2. Page: _____

The series I found: _____

_____

Practice Look at these sentences and decide which sentences have a series in them and need commas. Some sentences do not have a series. Place the commas where they are needed.

1. The bread is crusty and good.

2. Jo rode on a tractor a horse and a truck at the farm.

3. Tameka felt happy rested and silly after camp.

4. The puck flew across the ice hit my skate and stopped inside the net.

5. My mother is a doctor a teacher and a cook.

Apply Make up your own sentences, using commas to separate a series of three or more.

1. In my tool box, I have _____

_____

2. I dressed in _____

_____

3. My pet is _____

_____

Words Ending in -*il*, -*al*, -*le*

Focus: Words that end with the same sound can be spelled different ways. If you are not sure which spelling to use, find the word in a dictionary or ask for help.

One way to learn the spelling of a word is to look at the word and picture it in your mind. Then, remember how it is written.

- Some words have *il* in the last syllable:

  fossil, council.

- Other words have *al* in the last syllable:

  equal, animal.

- Another group of words has *le* in the last syllable:

  gentle, candle.

Identify Find examples of words ending with *il*, *al*, or *le* in an unstressed syllable from "The Story of the Statue of Liberty." Write your words on the lines below.

_____

_____

_____

Words Ending in -il, -al, -le *(continued)*

Practice and Apply In the sentences below, underline the words with the unstressed ending and write the *il, al, le* ending in the space provided. Notice the sound of the ending. The first sentence is done for you.

1. When I tell a <u>riddle</u> to my friends, they laugh. **le** _____

2. My favorite sweater has purple stripes. _____

3. I have a pencil and two pens. _____

4. The star seems to sparkle at night. _____

5. The medical team helped the sick people in

   the hospital. _____

6. If I win the raffle, I will get a great red bike.

   _____

7. My favorite animal is my dog Patches. _____

8. The logical way to do well on your test is to study and get a

   good night's sleep. _____

Multisyllabic Words

Focus A syllable is a word or part of a word with only one vowel sound. Multisyllabic words are words with more than one syllable.

Examples:

- two syllables: *num-ber, cor-rect, read-ing, tur-tle*

- three syllables: *syl-la-ble, um-brel-la, al-pha-bet*

- four syllables: *ed-u-ca-tion, A-mer-i-can, li-brar-i-an*

Identify Look through "The Story of the Statue of Liberty" to find multisyllabic words. Write the words on the lines below. Then write how many syllables the word has. The first one is done for you.

Word	Number of Syllables
1. beautiful	3
2. _____	_____
3. _____	_____
4. _____	_____

Practice Read the list of words. Then write the number of syllables in each word on the line provided. The first one is done for you.

addition   __3__   freedom   _____

friend   _____   drink   _____

unhappy   _____   together   _____

independence   _____   crown   _____

happy   _____   construction   _____

disappointment   _____   telephone   _____

Apply Write three sentences. One sentence should contain a one-syllable word, one should contain a two-syllable word, and one should contain a three-syllable word. Underline these words in your sentences.

1. _____

_____

2. _____

_____

3. _____

_____

Special Spellings
/aw/: *all, alk, augh, ough*

Focus The /aw/ sound is most often spelled *aw* or *au* as in *paw* or *pause*.

> The /aw/ sound you hear in *ball* can be spelled *-all*, *-alk*, *-augh*, and *-ough*.
>
> ### Examples
>
> | | | | |
> |---|---|---|---|
> | all | ball | augh | taught |
> | alk | walk | ough | bought |

Practice Read the following passage. Circle the letters that spell the /aw/ sound.

> The tall man coughed as he walked and thought that he caught a cold. His small daughter talked beside him on the sidewalk. She brought a ball with her.

Write each word under the correct spelling pattern.

SPELLING /aw/

-all	-alk	-augh	-ough
_____	_____	_____	_____
_____	_____	_____	_____
_____	_____	_____	_____

Apply Read the clues and choose the word from the box that answers the clue. Write the word on the line.

bought	small	chalk	fought
ought	cough	stalk	wall

1. not large　　　　　　　　　　_____

2. corn grows on this　　　　　_____

3. a sound you make
   with your throat　　　　　　_____

4. something you spent
   money on is this　　　　　　_____

5. write on the
   blackboard with this　　　　_____

6. a good place to
   hang a blackboard　　　　　_____

7. you should do　　　　　　　_____

8. fighters did this　　　　　　_____

Multiple-Meaning Words

Focus Some words have more than one meaning. To figure out the meaning that makes the most sense, look at other words in the sentence and use a dictionary.

Use the words in the sentence to figure out the meaning of the word.

I poured milk in the **glasses**.

I need **glasses** to read the chalkboard.

Identify Read these sentences about "New Hope." Write the meaning of the underlined word. Then write another meaning for the word. Use a dictionary to help you find other meanings.

1. Jimmy loved the statue in the <u>park</u>.

   _____

   park: _____

   _____

2. This looks like a good <u>place</u> to live.

   _____

   place: _____

   _____

Practice and Apply Read the different meanings for each word. Write the meaning of the word as it is used in the sentences.

1. **back:** to return something, take it back; a part of the body

   They couldn't take the dog <u>back</u>, so they adopted him.

   Meaning of **back:** _____

   He fell down and hurt his <u>back</u>.

   Meaning of **back:** _____

2. **broke:** not working; to have no money

   The axle on the wagon <u>broke</u>.

   Meaning of **broke:** _____

   The poor man was <u>broke</u>.

   Meaning of **broke:** _____

Name _____ Date _____

Subject-Verb Agreement

Focus Subjects and verbs must agree in all sentences.

- The subject and predicate *agree* when they work together.

    One **horse** <u>pulls</u> the wagon.

    Two **horses** <u>pull</u> the wagon.

- The subject of a sentence can have more than one noun. Compound subjects have two nouns joined by the word *and*.

    The red horse and the black horse <u>pull</u> the wagon.

Practice Circle the verb that agrees with the noun in the subject.

1. Jimmy (visit, visits) his grandpa.

2. Karen and Lars (start, starts) a new life in America.

3. Lars (buy, buys) a wagon.

4. Lars and Karen (need, needs) tools, food, and seeds.

Circle the noun in the subject that agrees
with the verb.

5. The (man, men) tells a story.

6. The young (boy and girl, boy) listen carefully.

7. The (story, stories) tells about how the
town began.

8. The (horse, horses and riders) stop to drink.

Apply Rewrite each sentence with a compound
subject. Be sure the compound subject agrees
with the verb.

1. Peter does his chores.

_____

_____

2. Mathilde plays with Fido.

_____

_____

3. The stagecoach stops here.

_____

_____

Name _____ Date _____

Spelling Vowel + *r* Words

Focus Learning the different spellings of the vowel plus *r* sound will make your writing clearer and easier to read.

- The vowel plus *r* sound can be spelled different ways. Some spellings are

  ar   *er*   *ear*   *ir*   *or*   *ur*

- Each spelling can have different sounds. Some sounds are:

ar	*er*	*ear*	*ir*	*or*	*ur*
share	here	hear	girl	for	hurry
park	her	heard	their	work	pour
	where	bear	weird		

Identify Look through "The Butterfly Seeds." Find and write words that have one of the vowel + *r* spellings.

_____ _____ _____

_____ _____ _____

_____ _____ _____

_____ _____ _____

Practice Look at the following list of words. Group them according to the vowel + r spelling at the top of each column.

share	butterfly	first	blurt
dirt	working	burlap	hurry
sisters	holler	yard	vendor
shirt	inspector	park	

-ar	*-er*	*-ir*	*-or*	*-ur*
_____	_____	_____	_____	_____
_____	_____	_____	_____	_____
_____	_____	_____	_____	_____

In the words you've written above, circle two words whose vowel + r sound is different from the others.

Apply Write two sentences using one word from the list above in each sentence.

1. _____

_____

_____

2. _____

_____

_____

Name _____ Date _____

Position Words

Focus The more you know about where things are in a story, the better you can picture what is happening in the story.

> **Position words** tell where things are. Some position words are *in, around, near, in the middle of, over, next to.*

Practice Look at the picture below. Then read each question. Use the position words to help you answer the questions.

outside of **next to** **in the middle**

1. Where is the table? _____

2. Where are the flowers? _____

3. Where is the butterfly? _____

Apply Read each sentence below.
Follow the directions.

1. Draw a house in the middle of the page.

2. Draw a flower in front of the house.

3. Draw a bee above the flower.

4. Draw a circle around the bee.

5. Draw a butterfly next to the bee.

6. Draw a rock at the bottom of the picture.

Abbreviations

Focus An abbreviation is a shorter way of writing a title or a word.

Some abbreviations end with a period.

Doctor Drake ⟶ Dr. Drake

Maple Street ⟶ Maple St.

United States of America ⟶ U.S.A.

Practice Complete each sentence.

| Mr. | Mrs. | Miss | Ms. | Dr. |

1. My teacher's name is _____.

2. The school principal is _____.

3. When I am sick, I go see _____.

4. _____ lives next door.

5. _____ lives nearby.

Apply Draw a picture of a grown-up you know. Write two sentences about the grown-up, using a title with his or her name.

_____

_____

_____

_____

Classifying and Categorizing

Focus A writer often includes many details in a story. **Classifying or categorizing** the information can help show how details are related.

> Readers sort information into different groups, or **categories**. This helps them to understand and remember what they read.

Identify Look at "A Very Important Day" to find where the immigrants came from. List all of the countries mentioned in the story. Then classify the countries into two groups: large and small.

1. **Countries:** _____

   _____

   _____

2.   **Group 1–Large**   **Group 2–Small**

   _____   _____

   _____   _____

   _____   _____

   _____   _____

Practice Make a list for each category below.

Things I like to do

_____

_____

_____

_____

Things I don't like to do

_____

_____

_____

_____

Apply Look at each item below. Think of two categories that might contain these items. Sort these items into the two categories. List your categories on the lines below.

subways   tractors   barns   skyscrapers
cows   fields   stores   sidewalks
many people   few people

_____   _____

_____   _____

_____   _____

_____   _____

_____   _____

Consonant Blends

Focus Sometimes two or three consonant letters stand for separate sounds that are blended together.

Here are some common consonant blends:

bl	block
cl	clamp
pl	play
br	bring
spr	spring
scr	screen

Identify Look through "A Very Important Day" for examples of consonant blends. On the lines below, write the word and underline the consonant blend.

1. _____

2. _____

3. _____

4. _____

5. _____

Practice and Apply Using the words in the box, fill in the blank with the correct word.

crash	train	plus	dress
street	stamp	swim	straight

1. Four _____ one equals five.

2. Did you buy a _____ for the letter?

3. The car _____ woke me up.

4. Your new _____ is very pretty!

5. Sheila just learned how to _____.

6. Please draw a _____ line on your paper.

7. The _____ was due at the station an hour ago.

8. Our _____ has seven houses for sale.

Name _____ Date _____

Time and Order Words

Focus The more you know about the time when things happen in a story and the order in which things happen, the better you can understand the story.

Time Words	Order Words
past	after
present	before
future	first
hour	last
day	then
year	finally

Identify Look through "A Very Important Day" for examples of time and order words. List two examples of each on the lines below.

Time Words

1. _____

2. _____

Order Words

1. _____

2. _____

Practice Have a discussion with your class about the sequence of events in your school day. Think about how events usually happen at certain times and in a certain order. Think about all of the things you do during a normal school day. Put each event on a separate index card. You may use the following list to help you.

Things I Do During a Normal School Day

school day continues

go to school

go home

lunch

start school day

Now put your cards in order. Think about why the cards should go in a certain order to make sense.

Apply Write a sentence about what you do after school. Underline the time and order words you have used.

_____

_____

_____

_____

Name _____   Date _____

Possessive Nouns

Focus A possessive noun is a noun that shows who owns something.

- Singular nouns show ownership by adding 's: *Robin's coat*
  the bird's wing
  Chris's shirt
- Plural nouns show ownership by adding only ': *cats' dishes*   *workers' hats*
  neighbors' houses
- Irregular plural nouns show ownership by adding 's: *people's wishes*
  men's shovels
  geese's flights

Identify Find examples of possessive nouns in the story "A Very Important Day." Write the examples on the lines below.

1. _____

2. _____

3. _____

4. _____

Practice In the following sentences, sometimes an 's is needed, and sometimes just an ' is needed to make the correct possessive. Fill in each blank. Underline what is owned in each sentence. The first one is done for you.

1. Efua_'s_ <u>camera</u> was used by a friendly stranger.

2. The new citizens__ friends were all at the courthouse.

3. The city__ snow made travel slow.

Apply Write a sentence with a singular noun showing ownership.

1. _____

_____

_____

Write a sentence with a plural noun showing ownership.

2. _____

_____

_____

Write a sentence using an irregular noun showing ownership.

3. _____

_____

_____

Fact and Opinion

Focus Writers talk to readers through their stories. To make their stories interesting, writers use facts and opinions.

> A **fact** is something that can be proven true. It is a fact that jalapeños grow on plants.
>
> An **opinion** is what someone thinks or feels. It is an opinion if someone says jalapeños taste good.

Identify Look back at "Jalapeño Bagels." Copy one sentence that gives a fact. Copy one sentence that gives an opinion.

Fact

1. _____

   _____

Opinion

2. _____

   _____

Practice Read this paragraph. Draw a line under each sentence that tells a fact. Circle the sentences that give opinions.

Jamie was born in the United States. His parents were born in Mexico. They moved to the United States ten years ago. His parents are wonderful. They have taught him how to speak two languages. It is important to know more than one language. That way he can talk to more people.

Apply Write several sentences about your favorite food. Make sure you include some facts and some opinions.

_____

_____

_____

_____

_____

_____

_____

_____

Plural Nouns

Focus Plural nouns name more than one person, place, or thing.

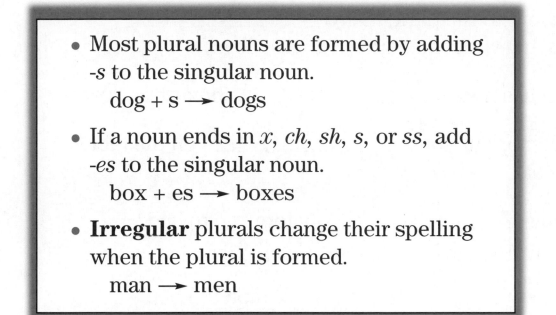

- Most plural nouns are formed by adding -*s* to the singular noun.

    dog + s → dogs

- If a noun ends in *x*, *ch*, *sh*, *s*, or *ss*, add -*es* to the singular noun.

    box + es → boxes

- **Irregular** plurals change their spelling when the plural is formed.

    man → men

Identify Look through "Jalapeño Bagels" for examples of plurals. Write your examples on the lines below.

_____   _____

_____   _____

_____   _____

_____   _____

Practice Read the sentences. Then choose the correct plural noun and write it on the line.

1. There were ten _____ at the party. (pizzas, pizzaes)

2. When I went to the park, many _____ were playing with each other. (doges, dogs)

3. My closet has many _____. (boxs, boxes)

4. Please do not put your _____ on the table. (foots, feet)

5. I brush my _____ before I go to bed. (toothes, teeth)

6. It took a few _____ of tape to keep the envelope sealed shut. (piecs, pieces)

Apply Write one sentence using one regular plural noun. Then write one sentence using one irregular plural noun.

1. _____

   _____

2. _____

   _____

Antonyms and Synonyms

Focus Antonyms are words that are opposite in meaning. Synonyms are words that mean the same or almost the same thing.

Antonyms

hot and cold	thin and thick	stop and go
hard and soft	in and out	up and down

Synonyms

small and little	sad and unhappy
happy and glad	cold and chilly

Identify Find examples of antonyms and synonyms from the story "Jalapeño Bagels." Write them in the spaces provided.

Antonyms

1. _____

2. _____

Synonyms

1. _____

2. _____

Practice Read the sentences. Underline the <u>synonym</u> of the **bold** word. The first sentence is done for you.

1. The baby is **unhappy**. <u>sad</u>   hungry

2. Bobby is very **tired**.   sleepy   hurt

3. The tiger looked **scary**.   frightening   ugly

4. The ant is **little**.   red   small

Read the sentence. Underline the <u>antonym</u> of the **bold** word. The first sentence is done for you.

5. The building is **tall**.   <u>short</u>   hot

6. The flowers are very **pretty**.   light   ugly

7. The forests are **thick**.   thin   soft

8. The tree's bark feels **rough**.   noisy   smooth

Apply Write a sentence using the **antonym** of the bold word.

night

_____

_____

Write a sentence using a **synonym** for the bold word.

small

_____

_____

The Parts of a Letter

Focus A friendly letter has five parts. It is important to use correct punctuation in a letter.

- The **heading** tells where the letter is from and the date the letter was written. Capitalize the first letter of proper nouns such as names, places, and dates.

- The **greeting** tells who receives the letter. Use a comma at the end of the greeting.

- The **body** is what the writer has to say. The first word in each sentence begins with a capital letter and each sentence ends with a punctuation mark.

- The **closing** ends the letter. It is above the name of the letter writer. The first letter of the first word is capitalized. Use a comma at the end of the closing.

- The **signature** is the name of the letter writer.

Practice Read the letter on the next page. Label each part of the letter in the space provided.

93 Broad Street   _____
Boston, Massachusetts
March 15, 1999

Dear Aunt Maryanne,   _____

    Thank you for coming to   _____
my birthday. The new
computer game you gave
me is so much fun to play!

Yours truly,   _____

Tom   _____

Apply Write a friendly letter of your own. Be
sure to include all five parts of the letter and to
use correct punctuation.

_____

_____

_____

_____

_____

_____